Travellers

Thomas
Cook
Publishing

GREEK ISLANDS

BY
ROBIN GAULDIE

Produced by
Thomas Cook Publishing

Written by Robin Gauldie

Original photography by Steve Day, Terry Harris, Rob Moore, Anthony Sattin and James Tims

Edited and designed by Laburnum Technologies Pvt Ltd,
C-533 Triveni Apts, Sheikh Sarai Phase 1,
New Delhi 110017

Published by Thomas Cook Publishing
A division of Thomas Cook Holdings Ltd

PO Box 227, The Thomas Cook Business Park,
Units 19–21, Coningsby Road,
Peterborough PE3 8XX, United Kingdom
E-mail: books@thomascook.com
www.thomascookpublishing.com

ISBN: 1-841572-54-3

Text © 2002 Thomas Cook Publishing
Maps © 2002 Thomas Cook Publishing
First edition © 2002 Thomas Cook Publishing

Managing Director: Kevin Fitzgerald

Publisher: Donald Greig

Series Consultant: Vivien Stone

Printed and bound in Spain by: Grafo Industrias Gráficas, Basauri

Cover: Kimis Theotokov Church, Santorini, Cyclades Islands.
Photograph by W. Bibikow/jonarnold.com
Inside cover: photographs supplied by Spectrum Colour Library

CD manufacturing services provided by business interactive ltd, Rutland, UK

Contents

Introduction

Variety is the spice of the Greek islands. Some visitors go in search of the ancient and medieval worlds of temples, castles, and fortresses. Others seek peaceful harbour or hilltop villages and secluded coves. Millions more are simply looking for a good time in bustling holiday resorts with sandy beaches, friendly tavernas, and discos. All of these are waiting to be discovered.

Typically, each island moves to its own rhythm. It has its own landscape, architecture, and traditions which, though they may have basic shared characteristics, are also distinct.

Through the long summer months, Greek islanders spend most of their time outdoors, though they avoid the fierce middle-of-the-day temperatures by staying indoors and taking a siesta, which is why many places resemble ghost towns during the afternoon.

For visitors, there is no better way to while away the hot afternoons than sitting at a shady harbourside table with a glass of cold beer, or a carafe of retsina and a plate of prawns or octopus landed fresh that morning.

You can stay in the bright, newly-built apartments and hotels of the popular resorts, seek out smaller pensions or village rooms in quiet hideaways, or find comfortably restored old homes, traditional shipowners' mansions, or secluded luxury hotels.

The Aegean and Ionian Seas offer some of the best yachting and windsurfing in Europe, in addition to waterskiing, parascending, diving, and snorkelling from dozens of beaches.

The Greek Islands

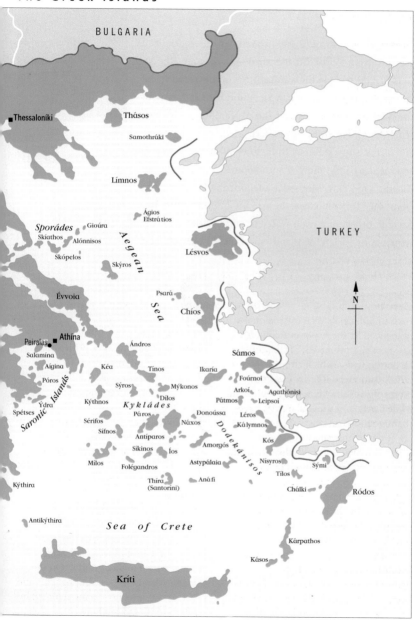

The Land

Greece claims some 2,000 islands, islets, rocks, and skerries, from Corfu, off the northwest coast, to Rhodes (and just beyond) in the southeast. Six of these, Corfu and its satellites, are in the Ionian Sea, a southern extension of the Adriatic. The rest clutter the Aegean Sea, with Crete separating them from the Eastern Mediterranean. Some are just a stone's throw from foreign shores: Corfu is separated by little more than a kilometre of water from Albania, and tiny Megísti (Kastellórizon) is only 500m from the Turkish coast. Many are mountainous and barren, others are well-watered and fertile, and the tremendous variety of island landscapes is part of their never-ending charm.

Sulphurous volcanic craters – the variation in island landscapes is one of the attractions.

Climate

Each island has its own microclimate, influenced by the sea, prevailing winds, and nearby landmasses. Spring comes earliest to Crete, which also has the hottest summers. Rhodes has more hours of sunshine than any other island, while Corfu and the Ionian isles have slightly milder summers. The Cyclades are swept by the gale-force *meltemi*, which can blow for up to three days at a time in summer. Sámos and the Northeast Aegean islands, close to the Turkish coast, have late springs, influenced by the snowy heights of the Anatolian plateau. From late May to October, rain is rare.

Economy and Population

About 1.3 million Greeks are islanders, living on 169 inhabited islands. Many of these have only a handful of natives, such as tiny Maratho with just five people.

On the other hand, Crete is home to more than half a million. Tourism is a big employer on many islands, but fishing and farming are still important. Quarrying for marble and pumice is also a contributor to several island economies. Then, of course, there is the money sent home by Greeks living overseas that helps many families to manage.

Farming

Oranges, lemons, vines, and, above all, olives, grow abundantly on the more fertile islands. On smaller, drier isles, barley and wheat grow on terraces, and goats graze on higher ground. On the remoter islands, age-old implements and practices are only now being replaced by modern tools and methods.

Fishing

Island fishermen seek squid, sardines, mackerel, red mullet, and other prizes. The Aegean has been fished intensively for millennia and catches are getting smaller, but demand is high and prices are increasing.

Flora and Fauna

Many of the islands are rewarding for snorkellers and birdwatchers, and a rich insect and reptile fauna includes species found nowhere else in Europe. Rare sea turtles nest on some island beaches (*see pp42–3*). Wild flowers provide a blaze of spring colour (*see pp148–9*).

Geology

Some islands are of porous limestone rock; others, like Sámos, Samothráki, or Ikaría in the Aegean Sea are granite outcrops. Santoríni's unique landscapes are the result of millennia of volcanic activity, and Nísyros too has a slumbering volcanic crater. Marble is quarried on Páros and Thásos, and quarries on Mílos and Thíra (Santoríni) produce cement.

The Sea

In ancient times, the sea linked the islands with the empires of the Middle East. In the 15th and 16th centuries, the sea spelt prosperity for some but, at the same time, peril for others from pirate raids. Greek island captains controlled the wealthy trade of the Ottoman Empire, and during the War of Independence turned their guns on the Turks.

The sea also unites the scattered islands and provides a living for thousands of sailors and fishermen. Small sailing brigs (*caïques*) were the trade lifeline for many islands well into the 20th century, and every island has its quota of old salts from the Greek merchant navy.

The sea also provided an emigration route for islanders, most of them heading for the USA, Australia, Canada, and South Africa. However, ties with the islands proved difficult to break, and many Greeks settled abroad still bring their families 'home' in the summer for a nostalgic visit.

Deep natural harbours on many islands have helped shape Greece as a maritime nation

History

'The isles of Greece, the isles of Greece! Where burning Sappho loved and sung, Where grew the arts of war and peace, Where Dilos rose and Phoebus sprung, Eternal summer gilds them yet, But all, except their sun is set.'

GEORGE GORDON, LORD BYRON
(1788–1824), *Don Juan*

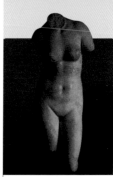

Exhibit from the Iraklion
Archaeological Museum

3000 BC	Seafaring Bronze Age trading culture develops in Cyclades.
2200–1700	Early Minoan civilisation in Crete develops into Minoan palace culture and trade empire.
1600	Mycenaean culture spreads to islands from Greek mainland.
c.1470	Explosion of Thíra volcano. Collapse of Minoan civilisation.
1200	Waning of Mycenaean culture.
c.1000	Arrival of Dorian Greeks in Aegean islands.
800–600	City-state system emerges.
490	First Persian invasion. Athenian victory at Marathónas.
480	Second Persian invasion. Persian fleet destroyed at Salamis.
479	Persian defeats on mainland end Persian wars.
478	Athens dominates the islands as leader of Delian league.
431–404	Peloponnesian War between Sparta and Athens ends in Athenian defeat.
358–336	Rise of Macedonia.
336–323	Reign of Alexander the Great.
323–196	Era of Macedonian kings.
215–146	Wars with Rome, culminating in Roman conquest.
1st century BC	Pompey clears pirates from Aegean islands.

AD **260–8**	Gothic fleets raid islands.
330	Roman Emperor Constantine moves his capital to Byzantium (Istanbul), renaming it Constantinople and founding the Christian Byzantine empire.
600–900	Arab corsairs conquer Crete, sack Rhodes, and raid Aegean islands.
960–61	Byzantine general Nikiforos Fokas recovers Crete.
1204	Frankish/Venetian Fourth Crusade sacks Constantinople. Venetians take Crete, the Ionian islands, and Evia. Knights of St John take Rhodes, Kós, and the Dodecanese. Cyclades come under rule of the Sanudo Dukes of Náxos, vassals of the Frankish King of Athens. Genoa acquires Northeast Aegean islands.
1354–1453	Turkish conquest of Byzantine Empire ends in fall of Constantinople.
1499–1530	Turks conquer Venetian strongholds on mainland.
1522	Turks take Rhodes.
1566	Turks conquer Chíos and Náxos.

1571	Turks checked at sea-battle of Lepanto by Holy League led by Don John of Austria, but in same year take Sámos.
1669	Turks capture Crete.
1797	Revolutionary France seizes Corfu and Ionian islands from Venice.
1814–64	British protectorate of Corfu and Ionian islands.
1821–30	War of Independence. Cyclades and Argo-Saronic islands, with parts of the mainland, form the new Republic of Greece.
1831	Governer Capodistrias assassinated.
1833	Bavarian Prince Otto becomes King Otho I of the Hellenes (Greeks).
1864	Britain cedes Corfu and Ionian islands to Greece.
1866	Cretan revolt against Turkey fails.
1912	First Balkan War. Greece annexes Chíos. Italy seizes Rhodes and the Dodecanese from Turkey.
1913	Second Balkan War. Cretan revolt succeeds. Crete joins Greece after

brief independence. Many Cretan Muslims migrate to Rhodes. Greece annexes Lésvos, Sámos, and Ikaría.

1917	World War I. Greece joins Britain, France, and Italy.
1919	Encouraged by Britain and France, Greece lands troops at Smyrna (Izmir) in Turkey.
1920–3	War between Greece and Turkey ends in defeat for Greece. Around one million Greeks driven from Turkey.
1924–36	Political chaos. General Metaxas becomes dictator.
1940	Italian invasion defeated.
1941–4	German and Italian occupation of mainland and islands. Varied resistance groups active, especially on Crete. British commando raids on Dodecanese islands.
1946–9	Civil war on mainland, with the USA and Britain supporting the Royalist right-wing government forces against the left.
1947	Rhodes and the Dodecanese join Greece.
1953	Earthquake.
1967–74	Military junta led by Colonel George Papadopoulos rules Greece. King Constantine expelled. Referendum ends the monarchy.
1974	Collapse of the junta after the Turkish invasion of Cyprus. Restoration of democracy.
1981	Greece joins the European Community. Left-wing PASOK party led by Andreas Papandreou elected.
1985	PASOK re-elected.
1989	PASOK defeated. Series of short-lived caretaker governments.
1990	Nea Dimokratia party elected under Konstantinos Mitsotakis.
1993 & 97	PASOK re-elected.
1997–8	Tension between Greece and Turkey over ownership of uninhabited islands in the northeast Aegean.
1998–9	Greek public opinion strongly opposed to NATO bombing of Serbia.
2001	PASOK re-elected. Greece enters the Euro-zone.

The Acropolis of Rhodes

ISLAND DWELLERS
The Cyclades in the Bronze Age
The first metal-using civilisation in
Greece flourished in the Cyclades
around 3000 BC, leaving behind bronze
tools and implements, and remarkably
modern-looking carvings.

The Minoans
For five centuries, from around 2200 BC,
the Minoan empire based on Crete was
the greatest power in the Aegean,
exacting tribute from mainland Greek
princes and controlling colonies
throughout the Cyclades.

The Mycenaeans and Dorians
As Minoan power waned, the warlike,
bronze-using Mycenaeans (of Homer's
sagas) expanded from the mainland into
Crete and the Cyclades. Around 1100 BC
they were followed by the first Greek-
speaking, iron-using Dorian settlers.

The Classical Era
In the city-state era many of the islands
possessed powerful navies and merchant
fleets, and often vied with Athens for
control of Greek seas. Several sided with
Persia during the Persian Wars. At the
height of its power, Athens controlled
the Delian League of island states (those
surrounding the sacred island of Dílos),
but many of the islands aligned
themselves with Sparta against Athens
during the Peloponnesian Wars.

Alexander and His Heirs
With the rise of Macedon, the islands
came under the sway of Alexander and
his successors, and the Ptolemies of
Egypt used Thíra as a naval base.

The Romans
In 229 BC, Corfu and the Ionian group
became the first Greek islands to fall to
Rome. However, by the time Roman
subjugation of Greece was completed,
with the conquest of Athens in 86 BC,
many of the Aegean islands had become
pirate havens. The situation got so bad
that in the 1st century BC, the Roman
general Pompey raised a fleet to clear
the outlaws from the sea.

The Byzantine Empire
The power of Constantinople waned in
the 7th and 8th centuries and Arabs
from Spain conquered Crete, sacked
Rhodes, and raided the Aegean islands.
In AD 960–61, the Byzantine general
Nikiforos Fokas reconquered Crete, but,
by the 11th century, the Normans of
Sicily and the Venetians were raiding the
Ionian islands.

Venetians, Genoese, and Crusaders
Venice, with its eye on the Greek islands,
encouraged its Frankish allies of the
Fourth Crusade to sack Constantinople
in 1204. The Venetians then seized
Évvoia (Evia), the Ionian islands, Crete,
and bases on the mainland. The
Cyclades became the Duchy of Náxos,
ruled by the Venetian Sanudo family,
and the Dodecanese were taken by the
Knights of the Order of St John, who
also fortified Rhodes and Kós. Genoa
acquired the Northeast Aegean islands
through the marriage of a Genoese
prince to a Byzantine princess.

The Turks in the Greek Islands
The Turkish conquest of mainland
Greece, except for a few Venetian

strongholds, was complete by 1460, but the islands held out for much longer. Crete did not fall until 1669 and Tínos held out until 1715. Corfu was threatened, but remained part of the Venetian Empire until conquered by France in 1797. Turkish rule was a mixture of brutality and negligence. Many seafarers grew rich on the sea-trade of the Ottoman Empire (which the Greeks controlled), but islanders who rebelled against the Sultan were massacred.

The British in the Ionian

Britain ousted the French from Corfu in 1814, and the seven Ionian islands remained in British hands until 1864, when they were handed back to Greece.

The Italians in the Dodecanese

Italy seized the Dodecanese from Turkey in 1912, making Rhodes the provincial capital and Léros the eastern base of the Italian navy. The Italians restored the Palace of the Grand Masters and the fortifications of Rhodes and left behind many ornate public buildings. When Italy surrendered in 1943, its Aegean possessions were occupied by the Germans and there were destructive raids by British commandos. It was in 1947, that the Dodecanese at last became part of Greece.

Beautifully sculpted statues at the Archaeological Museum, Iraklion

Governance

Since 1974, Greece has been a parliamentary democracy with an elected president whose role is mainly ceremonial. Real power is in the hands of an elected prime minister. Islanders share the nationwide passion for politics, and general elections take on a festive air of family reunion. The Civil War of 1946–9, fought on the mainland, had less impact on islanders, but memories of oppression then, and during the 1967–74 military junta, are still quite fresh.

A KKE poster urges Greece to pull out of the European Union

Oil and Troubled Waters

Also fresh in the memory is the Turkish invasion of Cyprus in 1974. Since small oil reserves were discovered in the northeast Aegean, Turkey has claimed mineral rights below the continental shelf. This, like anything which touches on Greek sovereignty, is a live political issue, and the substantial Greek military presence on islands near the Turkish coast is a constant reminder of the friction between the countries.

Political Parties

The Vouli ton Ellinon (Greek parliament) has 300 members, elected for a 4-year term by a system of reinforced proportional representation in 51 multi-seat constituencies, and 5 single-seat constituencies.

Political power is highly centralised, and islanders almost always feel that they are not getting a fair share from Athens when it comes to investment in infrastructure. This resentment is sometimes fuelled by rash campaign promises along the lines of 'vote for us and we'll build you an airport!'

Greece has two major political parties, the right-wing Nea Dimokratia (New Democracy) and the left-wing PASOK (Pan-Hellenic Socialist Alliance), and two smaller parties, the old-style KKE (Greek Communist Party), and a reformed KKE offshoot, Sinaspismos (Coalition).

There's as much variety in island politics as in every other aspect of life. Ikaría and Lésvos remain strongly left-wing despite the decline of the Communist Party elsewhere in Greece, while others lean to the right.

The national flag

Parliament Building at Syntagma Square, Athens

Culture

Visitors to the islands may still see grain being winnowed on a stone threshing floor and bread being baked in a wood-fired oven. Mules and donkeys are still vital load-carriers for farmers on steep hillsides.

Greeks talk with their hands, and conversation is always animated

These days, though, the grain will not have been ground in an island mill. The surviving windmills in places such as Mýkonos have become chic holiday homes, and flour for the bakeries comes from big mills on the mainland.

Boats and Planes

Big, fast, modern ferries, high-speed hydrofoils, and jet aircraft have taken the place of the *caïques* and steamers of the old days, bringing the islands closer to the mainland and the outside world. Islands with international airports or domestic flights to Athens are the envy of those without, and charter flights are seen by every islander as the key to a fast tourism fortune.

The Tourism Boom

Charter flights now go straight to a dozen holiday isles from the big cities of Europe, bringing up to 11 million tourists a year to the beaches of their dreams. Islanders who once scraped a bare living from handkerchief-sized fields and thorny goat pasture now grow prosperous from holidaymakers; jobs are created, and there is far more incentive for young islanders to stay at home, instead of seeking a livelihood elsewhere. Moribund villages have been reborn and tottering houses rebuilt.

Change for the Better?

Have all the changes been positive? Most definitely not. Once-tranquil havens are lined with noisy bars and discos, unsilenced motorbikes boom down narrow streets, and thriving resorts have mushroomed on unspoilt island beaches. The tourism season is mostly summer only, and competition for tourist revenue in peak season can be intense and unseemly.

That said, the islands remain very special. There are still hundreds of spots away from the crowds, and Greek islanders remain among the most charming people in the world. Even on the most developed island, a short journey inland, away from the smell of suntan oil and the beat of the disco takes you back to villages and landscapes largely unaffected by the holiday boom.

Islanders Overseas

Millions of Greeks left their homeland during the 19th century, and many islands which once numbered their inhabitants in tens of thousands have quite literally been decimated. Migrants from any one island tended to head for the same destination, and almost all dreamed of returning when their fortunes were made. Not all succeeded, but on Sámos and Kýthira you will hear lots of Greek-Australian accents; Kálymnos and Chálki have links with Florida; Ikaría and Lésvos with the USA and Canada; on Kárpathos you may meet Greek returnees from Kenya and Sudan.

Island Personality

People who have met Greeks overseas hustling to make their fortune are sometimes surprised to see how laid-back they seem to be in their natural habitat. That is partly because much of the hard work of an island day is done in the early morning hours, when most visitors are still asleep. Partly, too, islanders are blessed with a sunny mentality that takes life as it comes, though they can drive a hard bargain when they want to.

Ancient Ancestors?

You may well meet Greeks bearing ancient names – Aristotle and Socrates are popular – but unsurprisingly, modern Greeks have not much in common with their ancestors of more than 2,000 years ago. There is a real pride in their achievements, but if Greeks do look back on a Hellenic Golden Age, it is the 1,000-year Byzantine Empire of Constantine the Great and his heirs.

On smaller, less prosperous islands such as Síkinos, traditional farming methods are still practised

Impressions

You will find relics of the ancient world scattered throughout the islands. Some carefully signposted sites have little more than a few scattered column-drums or foundations to mark them, and all have suffered the ravages of up to 4,000 years of natural disasters, war, invasion, and neglect.

A craggy hillside hides a castle at Kýthira

Crete and the Aegean island groups offer the richest treasure trove. Sites guaranteed not to disappoint include Knosós, Faistós, and Górtys on Crete *(see pp80–81);* Líndos, Ialýssos, and the Temple of Apollo on Rhodes *(see pp102–7);* the Agorá and Asklipion on Kós *(see pp110–11);* the Sanctuary of the Great Gods on Samothráki *(see pp124–5);* Akrotíri on Thíra (Santoríni) *(see pp68–9),* and, perhaps, most of all, the complex of shrines and sanctuaries on Dílos *(see pp61–3).*

A specialist guidebook or guide who knows the area is vital if you want to make the most of your sightseeing, helping the mind's eye to see the palaces and temples as they once were.

Beaches

The Greek islands offer every kind of beach, from tiny, hard-to-reach coves of white pebbles to sweeps of sand lined with loungers and parasols. There are long sandy beaches on Corfu and its Ionian neighbours, Zákynthos and Kefalloniá, on Páros and Mýkonos, on the north coast of Crete, and on Rhodes, Sámos, and Kós. Thíra (Santoríni) has beaches of black volcanic sand (which can get painfully hot under the mid-

summer sun). Best of all, perhaps, is popular Skíathos, with many beaches.

Castles

Venetians, Turks, Genoese, and Crusaders left crag-top castles towering over key harbours everywhere. Some, like those on Corfu and Léros, are still used by the Greek military. Among the most impressive are Kýthira's Venetian keep, the castles of the Gattelusi on Lésvos, the fortresses of the Knights of St John on Kós, and the fortified Monastery of St John the Divine on Pátmos.

Historic Towns

The Old Town of Rhodes, with its massive fortifications, labyrinth of alleys, and restored palace, is the most striking of all the island capitals. Chaniá and Réthymno on Crete, and the island capital on Kós, are all interesting blends of ancient and medieval history with an exotic whiff of the East. Náxos Town, the capital of Náxos, with its whitewashed, hidden citadel of the Sanudo dukes, is another delight. Corfu Town offers a different history, with reminders of Venice, revolutionary France, and Victorian England.

Picturesque Villages

The boxy white houses and blue-domed churches of so many postcards are found in the Cyclades group. The island capital almost always bears the name of the island itself, though islanders usually just call it Chóra (the market-village). The prettiest include the dramatic crater-edge Chóra on Thíra (Santoríni), the harbourside Chóras of Mýkonos and Páros, and the hilltop Chóra of Folégandros. Astypálaia and Amorgós are lovely white villages, too.

For a taste of a different village style, visit Mólivos on Lésvos with its tall, Turkish-style homes, the Argo-Saronic islands and their sea-captains' mansions, or Líndos on Rhodes with its pebble-mosaic courtyards.

When to Go

The islands are most crowded in July and August. To avoid the crowds and the scorching heat, visit from mid-April to mid-June, or in September and early October. Spring brings the added beauty of red, yellow, and purple wild flowers, and in September the sea is still deliciously warm. The weather stays quite balmy into November, but it does become wet and windy. Most tourism facilities close by the end of October, though many smaller, up-market hotels now stay open all year.

Greek island beaches range from vast sweeps of sand to tiny pebbly coves

Island to Island

The arrival of the ferry is the high point of the day in a harbour village, and as an ant-like parade of backpackers and locals pours off the boat, accompanied by much shouting, gesticulating, and sounding of horns from a cavalcade of trucks, cars, and motorcycles, chaos seems to reign. In fact, it is all very organised, and allowing for wind and weather, it is surprising how punctual most ferries are. Timetables are issued close to the beginning of the tourist season, though they can be difficult to get hold of outside Greece. Thomas Cook publishes an Independent Traveller's guide to the Greek islands, *Greek Island Hopping* by Frewin Poffley, which gives schedules for every ferry service, descriptions of the ships, detailed maps, and sightseeing information about the islands.

Buying a Ticket

Harbourside agencies sell tickets, but each agency represents a different line. Where several lines operate, fares will be much the same but schedules differ, and the agency is unlikely to tell you about the services of a competing ferry. Ask around to be sure, or inquire at the Port Police office (*Limenarchion*), where an up-to-date timetable is displayed. Port police officers wear natty white uniforms. If you plan to island-hop, always allow for delays: strong winds can stop sailing for 24 hours or more and ferry schedules change every month.

Ferry, Hydrofoil, or Catamaran?

Main-line ferries are big, fast, and modern, with Pullman-seated lounges

Riding rented motorcycles and mopeds without helmets and protective clothing is risky

available for passengers buying the cheapest fare (still often, and misleadingly, called 'deck class'). Shorter hops may be served by smaller ferries with fewer facilities, but drinks and snacks are always available on board. Hydrofoils offer a speedy, costlier alternative on many routes in summer, especially in the Dodecanese, Argo-Saronic Cyclades, and Spozades groups. Fast catamarans also run from Rhodes to several of the Dodecanese islands. But both of these types of vessel may provide quite a rough ride as they bounce across the tops of the waves at high speed.

Flying

Olympic Aviation, the domestic carrier of Olympic Airways, operates flights from Athens to many islands and some inter-island flights. Fares are cheap, but delays are frequent. Olympic faces competition from privately owned airlines, including Air Greece, Axon (which may buy Olympic Aviation), and Cronus Airlines.

Getting Around
By Bus
The island bus, usually irregular and dilapidated but packed with islanders and visitors, is an institution. Buses go anywhere there is a road, but out-of-the-way villages may have only one bus a day, so beware of being stranded.

By Boat
On the most popular holiday islands, small motorboats ply between the main villages and resorts, and the best beaches. Self-drive motorboats can be hired on some islands, including Corfu and Skíathos.

By Car
Cars, beach-buggies, or jeeps can be hired almost everywhere. Car hire in Greece is relatively expensive, and soft-top cars cost more. Roads are often rough and care is needed on the many sharp bends and steep hills. Make sure your vehicle insurance covers all damage (though damage to the underside and to tyres will always be your responsibility).

By Bike
Bikes are available for hire on some islands and are ideal for short trips. Longer journeys can be hilly and hot.

Hitch-hiking
Islanders are quite generous with rides, but you may have to wait for hours where vehicles are few.

By Moped and Motorcycle
Thousands of holidaymakers are injured, and some are killed each year riding rented motorcycles. These are often under-maintained, and few operators offer helmets or basic instruction. Island roads and island traffic are dangerous to the inexperienced rider. If you have not ridden before, it is advisable not to start here.

By Taxi
Taxis are quite cheap and are a very useful way of getting around. They await each ferry and are quickly snapped up. Be first ashore (you'll have to be pushy!) to be sure of getting one.

Admire the riches of the sea-world from a glass-bottomed boat

Manners and Customs

Island hospitality is legendary. Away from the boom-town resorts, you may be surprised by a carafe of retsina sent to your table by a complete stranger, or a gift of fruit from an island orchard. However, in the most popular resorts *philoxenia* ('love of guests') is vanishing, though slowly, as the tourism-profit motive asserts itself.

Queuing

Queuing for transport is unheard of. Boarding a bus or a ferry is a race for seats, and disembarking is a scramble for waiting taxis. In banks or post offices queues do form, though some Greeks will still push in ahead of tourists.

Dress Code

Topless sunbathing is now accepted on even the most public beaches. Nudity, however, is illegal. It is sanctioned on designated beaches, but it will offend on a town or resort beach. Shorts and T-shirts are acceptable summer wear everywhere, but knees and arms must be covered when visiting monasteries.

Women Travellers

Greek men nearly always feel that a woman is flattered by their attention, but an unambiguous 'no' is usually a sufficient deterrent to would-be Romeos. You are more likely to be harassed by mainland Greeks or foreign visitors than by islanders.

Language

The Greek language and alphabet can be intimidating, but a little Greek goes a very long way. Greeks believe that their language is almost impossible for foreigners to learn and knowledge of a few simple phrases will be extravagantly praised. English and German are widely spoken by islanders as a result of tourism, emigration, and service in the merchant navy.

Islanders use plenty of body language, which can be helpful or confusing. A backward jerk of the head, which looks like a nod, is actually a 'no', accompanied for emphasis by a click of the tongue. A rapid side-to-side shake of the head means anything from 'I don't understand' to 'What can I do for you?'

Η ΠΑΤΜΟΣ ΕΙΝΑΙ ΑΝΑΓΝΩΡΙΣΜΕΝΗ ΙΕΡΑ ΝΗ-ΣΟΣ ΣΥΜΦΩΝΑ ΜΕ ΤΟ ΝΟΜΟ 1155/81 ΤΗΣ ΠΟ-ΛΙΤΕΙΑΣ ΚΑΙ ΜΕ ΑΝΑΚΗΡΥΞΗ ΙΕΡΟΤΗΤΟΣ Α-ΠΟ Α.Θ.Π. ΟΙΚΟΥΜΕΝΙΚΟ ΠΑΤΡΙΑΡΧΗ ΔΗΜΗΤΡ ΙΟ ΤΗΝ 25/9/88 ΚΑΤΟΠΙΝ ΑΥΤΩΝ ΑΠΑΓΟΡΕ-ΥΕΤΑΙ Ο ΓΥΜΝΙΣΜΟΣ& Η ΑΠΡΕΠΗ ΕΜΦΑΝΙ-ΣΗ. ΠΑΡΑΚΑΛΟΥΜΕ ΣΕΒΑΣΘΕΙΤΕ ΤΑ ΝΟΜΙΜΑ.
ΙΕΡΑ ΜΟΝΗ ΙΩΑΝ ΘΕΟΛΟΓΟΥ
PATMOS IS A HOLY ISLAND ACCORDING TO LAW NO 1155/81 OF GREEK PARLIAMENT AND THE RESOLUTION OF PATRIARCH DEMETRIUS DATED 25/9/88 THEREFORE NUDISM & IMPROPER DRESS IS FORBIDDEN
THE MONASTERY OF ST. JOHN the THEOLOGIAN

Rules against nudity, topless sunbathing, and 'improper dress' are more often ignored than obeyed

Truly spectacular views can be had from the most unexpected places

Ióni a Nisiá
Ionian Islands

The Ionian islands stretch down Greece's west coast, from Corfu (Kérkyra) in the north to Kýthira, sitting alone off the southern tip of mainland Greece. The group includes several of Greece's most popular holiday isles, and it is easy to see why. Some of the country's best sandy beaches are to be found here, and the landscapes are greener and easier on the eye than those of many Aegean islands.

The beach at Agios Stefanos, Corfu

Reliable summer winds make the Ionians a favourite for yachting enthusiasts and windsurfers, while the green and hilly hinterlands appeal to walkers and explorers.

White walls at Avlemonas stand out against a barren hillside

Dramatic medieval harbour and hilltop fortresses make up for a dearth of more ancient sites, and the attractions of mainland Greece, within sight of each island, are easy to reach.

Ionian harbours and market towns bustle with colourful everyday life, and Corfu Town, the administrative capital of the group, is one of the most charming of island capitals. Unfortunately, earthquakes – the most recent in 1953 – have deprived the other Ionian islands of the type of picturesque village homes which delight visitors to other Greek isles.

There are seven main islands in the group, plus a scattering of tiny satellite islets, and Greeks often refer to them collectively as the Heptanissia (the Seven Islands). Six lie cheek by jowl in the northwest; Kýthira, the joker in the pack, is far away to the south. Although close to each other, these are not the easiest of islands for hopping, which often involves a zig-zag route, crossing to the nearest mainland port, taking a bus to another mainland harbour, then taking another ferry.

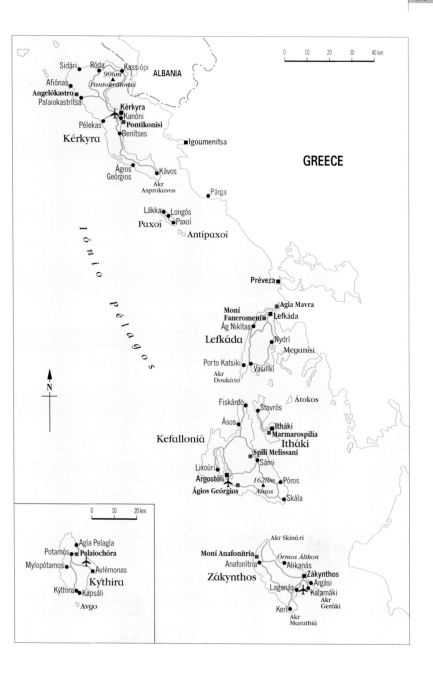

ANTÍPAXOÍ (Antipaxos)
See p38.

ITHÁKI (Ithaca)
Tiny Itháki (just under 100sq km) is best known as the legendary home of Odysseus (Ulysses) and his goal in his long journey home from the siege of Troy. Another famous visitor, Lord Byron (1788–1824), was so charmed by the island that he toyed with the idea of buying it.

Itháki is a narrow island, about 20 km long from north to south and cut almost in two by the Kólpos Mólou (Gulf of Molos). This opening on the east coast has sheltered waters and steady breezes which make the island a delight for dinghy-sailing, windsurfing, and other watersports. The island's sand-and-pebble beaches are small but uncrowded and usually clean.
2km east of Kefalloniá.

Itháki Town (Vathí)
Itháki's capital, home to over 2,000 of its 3,600 people, was rebuilt after the 1953 earthquake. Its charm owes more to its superbly scenic site, on a near-landlocked inlet surrounded by steep hills, than to any architectural merit.
At the inner end of a southern arm of the Gulf of Molos.

Marmarospilia (Cave of the Nymphs)
Odysseus is said to have hidden his treasure in this limestone sea-cavern.
3km southwest of Itháki Town.

Sarakiniko and Skinos
The best beaches on Itháki are between these headlands on the east coast, reached on foot or by small boats from Itháki Town.
2–5km northeast of Itháki Town.

KEFALLONIÁ
Made famous by the film *Captain Corelli's Mandolin*, and largest of the Ionian group, Kefalloniá is a near-tropical study in vivid turquoise, green, and brilliant white.

On the northwest coast, steep cliffs plummet down to white pebble beaches and the most brilliantly coloured blue sea in Greece, while the lower Kefallonián slopes are covered with citrus trees, olive groves, and vineyards. Robola wine, made from these grapes, is amongst the best in Greece.

The best beaches – long, sandy, and uncrowded – are on the south coast, where there are several small resorts. Like most of its neighbours, Kefalloniá suffered in the 1953 earthquake and most of its communities were rebuilt afterwards.

Ágios Geórgios
The hulking hilltop fortress of Ágios Geórgios stands guard over southern Kefalloniá. Built in 1300 by the Orsini family, the island's Venetian rulers, it was their capital until 1757, when they felt secure enough from Turkish invasion to move down to Argostóli. Its walls once sheltered 15,000 people, and the shells of houses and churches still stand within the imposing ramparts.
12km southeast of Argostóli.

Argostóli
The island's capital is on a natural west-

coast harbour sheltered by the Paliki peninsula. Entry is by a 650m causeway built in the early 19th century, when the island was ruled by Britain.

Moussío Arkheologiko (Archaeological Museum)

Interesting displays of pottery and other finds from around the island.
Veryoti 89. Open: Tue–Sun 8am–2.30pm. Admission charge.

Moussío Koryialeniou (Korgialenios Museum)

A collection of mock-ups of Venetian nobles' homes and artisans' workshops, as well as costumes and exhibits of life on Argostóli in another era.
Veryoti 41. Open: Mon–Sat, summer 9am–1pm & 6–8pm; winter 8am–2.30pm. Admission charge.

Fiskárdo

Named after the Sicilian Norman baron Robert Guiscard who died here in 1085, this pretty village, with its yacht-filled harbour, is the only survivor of the 1953 earthquake.
On the northern tip of the island, 53km from Argostóli.

Spíli Melissani (Melissani Cave)

A blue lagoon is fed by natural tunnels which stretch far beneath the island to emerge near Argostóli.
3km northwest of Sámi, on the east coast. Access by boat. Open: daily 8am–sunset. Admission charge.

The blue lagoon of Kefalloniá is fed by endless underground springs

KÉRKYRA (Corfu)

Corfu is an island of rolling green farmland, vineyards, and orange groves, all under the looming bulk of Mount Pantokrátoras. The second largest of the Ionian islands, it is by far the most popular – in fact, it is one of the most popular holiday islands in Greece, with resorts on every beach along its 217-km coastline. Most of these cater to the cheap and cheerful end of the package tour market.

The island capital, midway along the east coast, is delightful – and surprisingly untouristy, as it has no beaches of its own and most visitors stay at one of the resorts and visit the town only on a day trip. Inland, and in the island's farmlands and northern hills, quiet landscapes and rural villages are also quite untouched.

Corfu's most spectacular beaches and prettiest coastal scenery are on the island's long west coast. The heaviest development has been on the east coast, either side of Corfu Town and its airport, and you will find more space and solitude on the west, as well as glowing sunsets over the Iónio Pélagos (Ionian Sea).

Corfu is long and thin, and the grey slopes of the 906-m Mount Pantokrátoras dominate its wider northern end, with woods giving way to open hillsides. From these, and even from the east coast beaches, you have a clear view of the Píndos mountains on the Greek mainland, only a couple of hours away by boat, and of the even closer Albanian coast, which is less than a kilometre away from Corfu at its closest point.

Part of the Byzantine Empire from the 4th century AD, Corfu was seized by Venice in 1205 and stayed in Venetian hands, resisting several Turkish assaults, until 1797, when Napoleon conquered it for France. In 1814, France was ousted by Britain and the following year the island and its Ionian neighbours became a British protectorate. The Union Jack was hauled down in 1864 when the islands joined the Kingdom of Greece.

The Venetians left an Italianate island capital and a handful of Renaissance churches. The French bequeathed a

Colourful pedaloes and beach umbrellas brighten popular Ágios Geórgios beach

Kassiópi's harbourside and streets are lined with shops, cafés, and restaurants

stylish arcade of shops and cafés in Corfu Town, and the British legacy includes a collection of grand public buildings, and a taste for cricket and ginger beer.

Ágios Geórgios (North)

Just to be confusing, Corfu has two beaches officially called Ágios Geórgios, both on the west coast. However, this one, to the north, is better known as Ágios Giórgiou, which at least provides a slight differentiation. It is a great sweep of sand within a vast bay and is relatively undeveloped.
25km northwest of Corfu Town.

Ágios Geórgios (South)

This Ágios Geórgios, far to the south, is a giant expanse of majestic sand dunes with a number of new holiday hotels scattered along it. These are unenchanting, but the beach is so huge that it can offer solitude.
35km southwest of Corfu Town.

Kassiópi

A natural, lagoon-like harbour is the chief attraction of this fishing village-turned-resort on the north coast. Across the eastern strait are fine views of the rugged badlands of the Albanian mountains. The harbour is lined with cafés and restaurants. There are coves and beaches to either side, accessible by regular boat services.
30km north of Corfu Town.

Kástro (Castle)

The shattered walls of an early medieval Venetian castle sit on an easily accessed hillside just north of Kassiópi village centre, overlooking Kassiópi harbour.
Free admission.

Kávos

Set among gentle farmland, Kávos has mushroomed from a quiet fishing hamlet to a fully-fledged resort, with scores of bars and discos competing to offer the liveliest happy-hour and the strongest cocktails. The huge 2- to 3-km sweep of east-facing beach, with its gently-shelving sands, is the principal attraction during the day.
45km south of Corfu Town.

Kérkyra (Corfu Town)

The charming island capital has a population of around 40,000 and, with its faded rose and ochre stucco buildings, complete with wooden shutters, wrought-iron balconies, and flights of stone steps, it has a very Italian appearance. Periods of occupation by the British and French have also left their mark. The picturesque Campiello quarter was built during the Venetian era, on a headland guarded by two fortresses. It rises south of the ferry harbour, with the open space of the Spianada park on its east side, the Palaio Frourio (Old Fortress) on an eastern crag, and the Neo Frourio (New Fortress) to the north, near the harbour.
East coast of Corfu.

Arkheologiko Moussío (Archaeological Museum)

Finds from local sites. Highlights include the Gorgon from the Temple of Artemis and a 7th-century BC stone lion.
Vraila 5. Tel: (0661) 30680. Open: Tue–Sun 8am–2.30pm. Admission charge.

Byzantino Moussío (Byzantine Museum)

Housed in a 15th-century church, the museum features icons dating from the

Cafés along the Spianada in Corfu Town have a Parisian flair

A vividly coloured icon of the sainted Byzantine empress Theodora adorns Corfu's cathedral

15th to 19th centuries.
Panagia tis Antivouniotissas, Arseniou 3. Tel: (0661) 38313. Open: Tue, Wed, Fri–Sun 8am–2.30pm.

Ágios Spiridon

Built in 1596, the church houses the silver-encased body of the island's patron saint, credited not only with saving Corfu from the plague in 1630 and invading Turks in 1716, but also from Italian bombs in World War II. It also features an elaborate painted ceiling.
Platía Ágios Spiridou. Open: daily. Free admission.

Mitropoleos

The cathedral in the old quarter, built in 1577, houses the coffin of the Byzantine empress Theodora, who was canonised in the 9th century.
Platía Mitropoleou. Open: daily. Free admission.

Moussío Solomos (Solomos Museum)

The former home of the Greek poet

laureate, Dionysos Solomos (1786–1857), with a small collection of memorabilia.
Arseniou 41. Open: Mon–Fri 5–8pm. Admission charge.

Neo Frourio (New Fortress)

This angular stone fortress, built between the 16th and 19th centuries, is still used as a Greek naval headquarters.
Overlooking the ferry harbour. Closed to visitors.

Palaio Frourio (Old Fortress)

This 16th-century castle on twin crags is severed from the city by a sea-moat. There are fine views from its highest turret, and on summer evenings it is used for dramatic sound and light performances (*see p165*).
Cross bridge east of Spianada.
Open: 15 May–30 Sep 9am–8pm.
Free admission. Sound & Light show: four times a week 8pm. Admission charge.

Palace of St Michael and St George (Museum of Asiatic Art)

The elegant 19th-century palace, built for the British governors and later used by the Greek monarchy, houses a collection of Oriental artefacts.
North end of the Spianada. Tel: (0661) 23124. Open: Tue–Sun 8.30am–3pm. Admission charge.

Rotonda

A 19th-century memorial in the classical Ionian mode to Sir Thomas Maitland who was the first British governor of the Ionian protectorate between 1815 and 1824.
South end of the Spianada.

Spianada

The most elegant square in the Greek islands, Spianada is lined on one side by an arcade of stylish cafés, built by the French in the 19th century. Look for the statue of Ioannis Capodistrias (1776–1831), Greece's first president. Cricket is still played on the huge green.
Centre of Corfu Town, 750m from the harbour.

Vlachérne

Postcards of this delightful, if very commercialised, monastery islet, linked with the Kanóni beach by a 25-m causeway, manage to exclude the airport runway.
Kanóni, 4km from town centre.
Open: daily. Free admission.
Donations welcome.

Palaiokastrítsa

Steep, pine-wooded slopes and limestone crags surround this gorgeous double bay, the prettiest scene on Corfu with two small, crowded beaches separated by a towering headland. Motorboat service from Palaiokastrítsa pier covers coves and beaches nearby.

Palaiokastrítsa has been a renowned beauty spot since the British occupation, when army engineers built the first road there from Corfu Town. Famous visitors included Edward Lear (1812–88), who made a number of sketches and watercolours of local scenes.
26km northwest of Corfu Town.

Angelókastro

On a giddy peak above the sea sits the shell of a Byzantine keep which hides a tiny whitewashed chapel. It is named not after the angels, but after Michael I Angelos, the 13th-century Byzantine Despot of Ípeiros (Epirus) and Corfu, who built it.
11km north of Palaiokastrítsa. Freely accessible.

Zoodochos Pigi Monastery

This 18th-century fortress-like monastery contains a miracle-working 12th-century icon of the Virgin. The rock on the horizon is said to be a pirate ship turned to stone by the Virgin to protect her monastery from raiders.
Ágios Nikólaos promontory. Open: daily. Admission charge (candle purchase obligatory).

Pantokrátor Óros (Mount Pantokrátoras)

This 906-m high massif dominates northeast Corfu. You can drive almost all the way to the top, leaving your car at Petáleia village and walking the last 2km on a rough footpath. Alternatively, the walk up from the prettily dilapidated hamlet of Perítheia takes 1–1½ hours. The superb panorama encompasses the whole island. The treeless slopes of Albania lie to the east; the southerly Píndos ranges extend into the Greek mainland.
25 to 30km north of Corfu Town.

Pontikonísi

Just offshore, this islet with its miniature monastery is on all the postcards. The promontory is said to be the petrified remains of the ship of the Homeric hero Odysseus, turned to stone by the angry sea-god Poseidon.
750m from Kanóni, 4km from Corfu

Town centre. Excursion boats daily from most resorts.

Róda

Midway along the north coast of the island, Róda has one of the best beaches in the area. As a result, it has grown into a rather sprawling resort, but it makes a pleasant base for exploring Pantokrátoras and the northern hinterland.

37km northwest of Corfu Town.

Sidári

Like Róda, Sidári has grown into an extensive resort, thanks to a long, sandy beach and warm, shallow water.

48km northwest of Corfu Town.

Canal d'Amour (Channel of Love)

According to local legend, the channel, a long, rocky inlet whose cliffs are eroded into weird shapes, guarantees a match to any young woman who takes a dip in it.

2km west of Sidári.

Elegant, modern bell tower of the monastery at Palaiokastrítsa

KÝTHIRA

Rocky and remote, Kýthira guards the channel linking the Aegean with the open Mediterranean, not far from the southernmost point of the mainland (it is administered with the Argo-Saronic group of islands). Its high, flat-topped outline is instantly recognisable to anyone who has seen the film *The Guns of Navarone*, for which it was a location.

Kýthira's westward aspects, with their clifftop views of an empty horizon, appear almost Atlantic. It is an empty island, all but 3,400 of its inhabitants having left for Australia at the end of the 19th century, and it feels bigger than its 278sq km. High sea-cliffs thrust up to a windswept plateau of thorn-trees, studded with dabs of cultivated greenery, and most of the upland villages are hidden in little sheltered valleys.

This is an island for anyone looking for peace and quiet – except in July and August, when it bustles with Greek-Australian emigrants visiting stay-at-home relatives.
20km south of Akr Maléas (Cape Malea), 60km north of Crete.

Agía Pelagía

The northernmost of Kýthira's two harbour-villages, this is the less interesting of the pair, with a narrow, gritty beach at the foot of its rocky hillsides. However, it does have more frequent ferry and hydrofoil connections to the mainland than the southern port.
18km north of Kýthira Town.

Kapsáli

It has clean beaches on two pocket-sized bays, a string of tavernas, and a row of pretty white houses with flower-filled gardens. It is overlooked by the magical silhouette of Kýthira Town. Out to sea is Avgo, the egg-shaped sea-rock said to be the egg from which Aphrodite, goddess

Kýthira's castle offers magnificent views of the island

of love and beauty, hatched.
2km south of Kýthira Town.

Kýthira Town

With its whitewashed houses and narrow, twisty streets, this lovely clifftop village belongs much more to the Cyclades than to the Ionian. The best place to admire its position is from below, at Kapsáli.
On the southern tip of the island.

Kástro (Castle)

The prettiest castle in the islands perches on Kýthira's highest point. Inside there are the picturesque shells of the inner keep, a couple of small churches, and half a dozen rusting iron cannon of Napoleonic provenance (three of them carrying British insignia). The view is uplifting, with Avgo close inshore and the outline of Kýthira's tiny and almost uninhabited satellite, Antikýthira, on the southern horizon. Just below the castle, a plaque marks the birthplace of the poet and Orientalist Lafkadio Hearne (1850–1904).
100m from the village centre, at the end of the main street. Free admission.

Mylopótamos

Hidden in a ravine below the level of the dry plateau, Mylopótamos is pleasantly green and secret, with a burbling stream tumbling into a cool, oasis-like grotto.
6km north of Kýthira Town.

Káto Chóra

The crest of Venice, the Lion of St Mark, is carved above the great gateway of this charming and neglected miniature fortress. Arched buildings within the

Kapsáli's two bays

square of battlements are gradually falling into ruin.
7km west of Mylopótamos.

Spíli Agía Sofia
(Cave of the Holy Wisdom)

The entrance to this chilly, hillside grotto was once a church and still carries Byzantine frescoes. Further in, the 250-m cave system is adorned with spikes and pinnacles of limestone.
3km from Mylopótamos. Open: summer only, 3–5pm. Admission charge.

Palaiochóra

The Byzantine island capital is spectacularly sited with 100-m high cliffs on three sides, hidden from the sea to protect it from raiders. This did not save it from sacking by the feared Turkish pirate Barbarossa in 1537, and it was never rebuilt. Its ruins include a small castle and the shells of dozens of churches.
3km east of Potamós, 15km north of Kýthira Town.

LEFKÁDA (Levkas)

Levkas means white, and the bare mountain slopes of the hinterland are indeed whitish, with only a few pine trees clinging to their higher flanks. Around and below the central mountains, Levkas is a verdant, pretty island, with fertile farmlands and hundreds of blue beehives scattered among the goat pasture.

Only 650m separate Levkas from the mainland, and the narrow strait is crossed by a swing bridge and a causeway guarded by fortifications.

The east coast of the island faces on to a broad, calm expanse of water sheltered by the mainland and the offshore island of Meganísi. One of the tiny wooded islets here was the former hideaway of the millionaire Onassis family. This is a favourite area for yachts and windsurfers.

The west coast is more rugged, with cliffs and steep slopes rising above a string of white sandy beaches formed by the pounding of winter storms.

In the turbulent Middle Ages, Levkas changed hands even more frequently than most Greek islands. It was fought over by the Normans of Sicily and the Byzantine empire in the 11th century, taken by the Venetians in 1331, and ruled by Angevin Franks from 1362 until 1467, when it became the only Ionian island to be occupied by the Ottoman Turks. In 1684, it was reconquered by Venice, and from then on shared the fortunes of its Ionian neighbours, with a brief interval of Russian control between 1807 and 1814. *35km from Áktio airport, 40km southwest of the mainland port of Préveza.*

Thick woodlands stretch down to the sea on Levkas's south coast

Ágios Nikítas

There are excellent beaches on either side of this tiny fishing village and resort. Small boats commute between Ágios Nikítas and its satellite beaches several times a day in summer. *On the west coast, 8km southwest of Levkas Town.*

Akr Doukáto (Petra Levkas)

The legendary poetess Sappho (c.600 BC) is said to have thrown herself from this dramatic 70-m high white cliff, as the victim of unrequited love. Traces of a 7th-century BC Temple of Apollo can be seen next to the lighthouse on the island's southern tip. *46km south of Levkas Town.*

Lefkáda (Levkas Town)

Levelled by the 1953 earthquake, Levkas Town has been patchily rebuilt and has an eccentric charm. The upper storeys of many houses are built of brightly painted corrugated iron (an anti-earthquake ploy). The town faces inland, away from its lagoon, and hardly feels like a harbour town. Instead, it is more like an inland farming village. Repeated earthquakes have left it with little of historic interest but a medieval castle

and monastery that lie nearby.
Northwest coast.

Agía Mavra

The 14th-century fortress of the Orsinis
is complemented by ramparts built in
1807 by the Russians, who briefly
occupied Levkas between the ousting of
France, and the British takeover.
*1km from Levkas Town, on the islet
midway along the causeway.*

Moní Faneromeni (Faneromeni Monastery)

This deserted monastery dates from the
16th century and still possesses its
wooden simantron, the heavy wooden
bar beaten with a hammer to call the
monks to prayer.
*3km southwest of Levkas Town on the
road to Ágios Nikítas.*

Nydrí (Nidri)

Midway down the east coast, Nydrí
stands on a mirror-like lagoon which is
punctuated by tree-tufted islands and, in
summer, covered with the white and
dayglo sails of yachts and windsurfers.
There are some pleasant walks in the
hilly farming country inland, and a long
narrow beach stretches in front of the
village.
17km southwest of Levkas Town.

Porto Katsiki

One of the most spectacular beaches in
all the islands, this white crescent of
coarse sand lies beneath a half-circle of
jagged cliffs. It can be reached by a
rough, nerve-wracking jeep road or,
more comfortably, by boat from Ágios
Nikítas.
40km southwest of Levkas Town.

The busy harbour of Porto Katsiki

PAXOÍ (Paxos)

Measuring only 25sq km, Paxos is the smallest of the Ionian islands. It is also the closest to Corfu and is, therefore, a favourite day-trip destination. Regular ferries also run to Párga, the attractive mainland port resort, less than two hours away by boat.

Paxos's low hills are entirely cloaked in the silver-grey of some 300,000 olive trees. Here and there among the groves, you can spot a ruined farmhouse or olive-mill. There is plenty of shade beneath the olives, and as the island is only 270m at its highest point, and 10km from end to end, it is a favourite for walkers. Beaches are pebbly and tiny, and dotted at frequent intervals round the island's 25-km shoreline. The island's three tiny villages are also on the coast.

Paxos has few claims to historical fame, but Mark Antony and Cleopatra are said to have spent their last night together here before he sailed to defeat at the hands of Octavian at the sea-battle of Actium (31 BC), 100km south of Paxos. *20km south of Corfu; 25km west of Párga on the mainland.*

Antípaxoí (Antipaxos)

Paxos's tiny satellite achieves the startling feat of making its bigger neighbour look both busy and cosmopolitan. A hundred or so inhabitants cultivate small, terraced vineyards, and a handful of tavernas make a good living in summer from day-trippers who come by boat from Paxos and Corfu. The beach at Vrikes, the island's tiny village, is crowded when the boats come in, but for a bit more solitude you can easily walk to a clutch of quiet pebble-and-sand coves on Antipaxos's south coast. *5km south of Paxos.*

Lákka

Two curving promontories almost enclose Lákka's beautiful natural harbour. Gentle morning breezes and strong, constant afternoon winds make it one of Greece's premier windsurfing training centres. There is a pebbly beach on the west side of the bay. *12km northwest of Paxos Town.*

Longós

Longós sits on an east-facing mirror-like lagoon. A handful of villas and

OLIVES AND ISLANDERS

The silvery leaves of olive trees seem to cover almost every square metre of Paxos. Olives are part of Greece's heritage, grown from the earliest times as part of the 'Mediterranean triad' which also included grapes and grain. Olive trees are very long-lived and are valuable heirlooms. Like earmarks on sheep, numbers and initials painted on the trunk identify the owner of the tree. A family may have dozens of trees scattered in ones and twos all over an island.

Trees are often owned independently of the land they grow on, and the landowner must allow access for harvesting and pruning. The olive tree yields more fruit if pruned annually, and the slow-burning trimmings make excellent winter firewood. In the old days, islanders made bowls, plates, and spoons from close-grained olive wood, which is still used in boat-building.

cafés crowd around the village square and narrow quayside from which café tables have to be moved when the daily bus wants to squeeze by. There are clean, pebbly coves south of the village.
10km north of Paxos Town.

Paxoí (Paxos Town/Gaios)

Half of Paxos's islanders, about 1,200 people, live in the island's main village, a perfect Italianate island capital on a miniature scale, built around a flagstoned dockside square with a church and campanile. It is hidden away from the open sea by two islets, Panagía and Ágios Nikólaos, so that its harbour channel is more like a sheltered lake.
On the northeast coast at the southern end of Paxos.

Longós is one of the prettiest places on Paxos

ZÁKYNTHOS (Zante)

After Corfu, Zákynthos is the most popular of the Ionian holiday islands, and it is not difficult to see why. Inland, the island is a pastoral chequerboard of green vineyards, fruit orchards, and groves of almonds, grain fields, and pastureland. In spring, when its hills and roadsides are ablaze with wild blooms, it is easy to see why the Venetians called it *Fior di Levante* – the Flower of the Levant.

Argási

The popularity of this crowded resort is hard to explain, as its beach, a narrow strip of sand mixed with shingle, does not come up to the standard of other sunbathing stretches on Zákynthos. However, there are lots of bars and tavernas, and several discos, which gives Argási a nightlife that runs noisy Laganás a close second.

Laganás

Zákynthos's southeast coast is a broad bight, with Kólpos Lagana (the Laganás Gulf) bounded by two rocky headlands, Akr Marathiá in the southwest and Akr Geráki in the east. Midway between the two is the tourism boom town of Laganás, which in a few years has grown from a tiny collection of fishermen's cottages to a thriving resort full of hotels, tavernas, and bars. East of Laganás, a superb sandy beach stretches for almost 4km to Kalamáki, a smaller resort spread out among fields behind the beach. Inland, a fertile triangular plain, enclosed by wooded hills to the north, stretches east and west.
10km southwest of Zákynthos Town.

Turtle Nesting Grounds

A 2-km stretch of dunes and beach has been set aside as protected nesting grounds for the endangered loggerhead turtles which lay their eggs here each year. Nests are protected by wire enclosures and must on no account be disturbed. *See pp42–3.*
1km east of Laganás, stretching towards Kalamáki.

Moní Anafonítria (Anafonitria Monastery)

A survivor of several earthquakes, the monastery (it's also a nunnery) has a pretty medieval bell tower with faded frescoes, and a cell claimed to have been the refuge of Ágios Dionissos, the island's patron saint.
40km northwest of Zákynthos Town.
Open: daily, except during prayer.

Órmos Álikon (Alikes Bay)

This is the second-best swimming and sunbathing location on Zákynthos after Laganás, and those in search of less crowded beaches may rank it even higher as it is far less developed. It stretches for several kilometres – sandy at the southeast end, pebbly as the bay bends northwestwards. Two low-key resorts, Alikes and Alikanás, are separated by a 2-km stretch of yellow sand at the southeast end of the bay.
Approximately 15 to 20km northwest of Zákynthos Town.

Zákynthos Town (Zante Town)

The island's port and capital is a cheerful mixture of post-1953 buildings and a couple of medieval survivors, including a Venetian castle which dominates the town and lends it character.

Northeast coast.

Ágios Nikólaos

The lovely 15th-century church was restored after the 1953 earthquake and is one of the prettiest of the Ionian islands.

Platía Solomou. Open: daily.

Kástro (Castle)

The mighty ramparts and turrets of the castle were strong enough to withstand not only the Turks but also earthquakes. It is one of the island's handful of surviving medieval buildings. On a clear day there is a good view of the mainland.

On the hilltop above the harbour.
Open: Tue–Sun 8.30am–2.30pm.
Admission charge.

Moussío Neo-Byzantino (Museum of Neo-Byzantine Art)

Works here include 15th- to 19th-century icons rescued from earthquake-demolished churches, and striking paintings from the 17th-century Ionian School. The artists of this movement, fleeing the Turkish conquest of Crete, combined traditional religious themes and Italian Renaissance influences in their painting.

Platía Solomou. Open: Tue–Sun 8am–2.30pm. Admission charge.

A statue of the poet Dionysius Solomou stands outside the Museum of Neo-Byzantine Art

Turtles on the Brink

The sweeping sands of the Gulf of Laganás (Kólpos Lagana) are one of a handful of nesting sites of the endangered loggerhead turtle (*Caretta caretta*). Unfortunately, the turtles, which also lay their eggs on beaches in Crete and Kefalloniá, nest on exactly the kind of long, sandy beaches that tourists covet. Mother turtles arrive to lay their eggs in early summer, and the babies hatch two months later. But there are many dangers: females on their way to and from the nesting sites may be injured by speedboats; vehicles driving along the beach compress the sand, making it hard for females to dig nests, or they crush eggs already buried; bright lights from waterside tavernas attract the hatchlings inland, where they die of thirst and exhaustion; sunloungers crush the sand, and the metal poles of parasols can smash buried eggs.

The Greek government has banned night flights from Zákynthos airport, just inland from the bay, and a long stretch of the beach between Laganás and Kalamáki has been set aside as a reserve. Powerboats are prohibited from travelling at more than six knots in a large sector of the bay, but this ban is, sadly, often ignored. Boatmen who cash in on the turtle craze by offering turtle-spotting cruises should be boycotted as these harass mother turtles on their way to and from the beach.

In the last 20 years the number of loggerheads nesting at Laganás has halved. At sea, they are vulnerable to nets, lines, and pollution, and since only one hatchling in a thousand survives to lay its own eggs, the odds are stacked against the species *Caretta caretta*.

Loggerhead turtles may have laid their eggs at Laganás for 80 million years. It would indeed be tragic if a mere 20 years of tourism were to finish them off. How you can help:

- No lights or noise on nesting beaches at night
- Don't leave litter on the beach or in the sea
- Don't put up sun umbrellas in the dry sand where the turtles nest
- Don't try to help the hatchlings reach the sea. Doing it themselves is vital to their development
- Don't disturb any nests you find
- Don't take powerboat rides in the restricted zone of the Laganás Gulf.

For further information contact: Worldwide Fund for Nature Greece, Asklipiou 14, 10680 Athens. *Tel: (01) 3634 661.*

Loggerhead turtles have nested on these beaches for millions of years, but today their numbers are dwindling

Cruise: Around Zákynthos

This cruise around Zákynthos offers spectacular coastlines, a view of the island's less accessible beaches, and a glimpse of Zákynthos's mountainous northern neighbour, Keffaloniá, on the horizon. Two or three boats leave Zákynthos harbour every morning in high season and tickets are sold by agencies at all the resorts, and by tour operator representatives.

The 60-km round trip takes about 7 hours, including stops for lunch and swimming.

In early summer the sharp-eyed may be lucky enough to spot metre-long loggerhead turtles on their way to the egg-laying beaches (see pp42–3) and there is always a chance of seeing dolphins, especially if the sea is particularly calm. Cold drinks are sold on board and lunch is usually included in the cruise price.

Leaving Zákynthos harbour, the boat turns north, rounding the headland where the Venetian castle sits, then heads northwest along the line of the island's coast. Akr Tripití (Cape Trypiti), the westernmost point of the Peloponnese mainland, can be seen on the eastern horizon.

1 Kástro (Castle of the Orsinis)

Above the harbour at Zákynthos stand the battlements of the medieval castle, built by the Orsini family, who ruled several Ionian islands in the Venetian era. That the castle survived the disastrous 1953 earthquake is testimony to the skill of its builders.

The boat cruises northwest, with the sands of Tsiliví beach on the port bow, and the hills and farmlands of northern Zákynthos above them.

2 Órmos Álikon (Alikes Bay)

Alikes Bay shelters some of Zákynthos's prettiest and finest beaches at its southern end.

3 Kianou Spílaio

The blue-water sea caves near the island's northernmost tip are Zákynthos's most striking natural attraction. A trick of the light makes the sea in and around the arched limestone caverns seem luminously blue. If you stop to snorkel you will find that underwater swimmers appear dyed blue too. *Rounding the northern promontory, the boat turns west. At this point, 1,628-m peak of Mount Aínos, the highest point on the Kefallonian coast, is clearly visible to the north.*

4 Smuggler's Wreck

Stranded on a half-moon beach of rough, white sand, hemmed in by sheer limestone cliffs, is the wreck of a Greek freighter which went aground in 1982, carrying an illicit cargo of cigarettes and liquor destined for Syria. Local tales say much of the cargo was never recovered.

The picturesque scene has been captured on a thousand postcards. *Most cruises stop at Smuggler's Wreck beach for lunch and for those who wish to swim, before returning to Zákynthos Town in the late afternoon.*

A perfect hideout – Smuggler's Wreck beach

Argo-Saronic Islands

The Saronikós Kólpos (Saronic Gulf) lies south of Athens and is sheltered to the north and west by the Isthmus of Corinth and the Attica peninsula. This is the busiest stretch of the Aegean, criss-crossed by millionaires' cruisers, yachts, liners, ferries, and merchant vessels.

The peaceful harbour at Spétses

The ruin-studded shores of the Argolid peninsula divide the eastern Saronic Gulf from the western Argolic Gulf (Kólpos Argolikós), which bites deep into the Peloponnese mainland. The Argo-Saronic is home to four principal holiday islands – Aígina (Aegina), Ýdra (Hydra), Póros, and Spétses, plus the two lesser known isles of Salamína (Salamis) and Agkístri (Angistrion), and many other unvisited rocks.

Only a hop away from Athens and its port of Peiraías, these islands are a refuge for Greek city dwellers as well as

holidaymakers. Many better-off Athenians have weekend homes here, and many more take advantage of the fast and frequent ferries and hydrofoils for a day's outing. Nevertheless, the islands are in many ways closer to the visitor's idea of a Greek idyll than many of those located in the Aegean's remoter reaches.

Salamína, the closest of the islands to Athens, is historically renowned, for it was in the straits between it and the mainland that Athenian *triremes* annihilated the Persian fleet in 480 BC. Nowadays, however, it has virtually become an industrial and residential suburb of Athens.

There are few vehicles on these islands, and the little harbours with their steep tiers of white shipowners' mansions and villas are very much as first-time visitors to the Greek islands imagine them. They have avoided the kind of holiday invasion which has swamped less prosperous island communities.

Aígina and its satellite Agkístri, in the middle of the Saronic Gulf, are the closest of the group to Athens. Póros, further south, is only a few hundred metres off the Peloponnese coast. Ýdra lies midway between the Saronic and Argolic waters, and Spétses is at the very tip of the Argolid peninsula.

Ýdra's picturesque harbour was once the base of wealthy sea traders

AGKÍSTRI

The tiniest of the main
Saronic islands, Agkístri
has a single sandy beach at
Skála, on its north coast.
Crowded in the Athenian
getaway season, it is quieter
than the other isles for the
rest of the year, and most
of its islanders earn their
livelihood through fishing
and farming.
8km west of Aígina.

AÍGINA (Aegina)

The biggest of the Argo-
Saronic isles, Aígina has a
fertile hinterland of small
farms, a small fishing
harbour where tiny boats
unload even tinier
whitebait, and one busy
resort. During the War of
Independence (1821–30),
Aígina Town was (for a
time) the first capital of
independent Greece.
25km south of Peiraías.

Agía Marína

Aígina's main resort,
busiest at weekends and in
Athens' mid-July to late-
August holiday season, is
on a landlocked bay with a
long, but usually crowded,
sandy beach.
On the east coast.

Naós Afaía
(Temple of Aphaia)

The loveliest and most
complete of surviving
Greek island temples. Built
between 480 and 410 BC,
25 of its 32 tapering
columns are still standing.
*9km east of Aígina Town.
Tel: (0297) 32398.
Open: Mon–Fri 8.15am–
5pm, weekends 8.30am–
3pm. Admission charge.*

Aígina Town

Aígina Town's charm lies
in its narrow lanes of pink
and whitewashed houses,
and its quayside cafés
overlooking the old-
fashioned fishing harbour
and ferry port. It is an
ideal spot for watching a
typical Greek island port –
chaotic activity when the
ferry arrives, slumbering
inactivity between sailings.
*On the west coast of the
island.*

Kolona
(Temple of Apollo)

A lofty, 8-m high, fluted
column marks the site of
the 6th-century BC Temple
of Apollo. Archaeologists
have uncovered stretches of
walls nearby from the same
period. A museum displays
finds from this and other
excavations, including
elegant fragments of
sculpture.
*Immediately north of the
town beach, about 750km*

THE ADMIRALS OF THE ARGO-SARONIC ISLANDS

When the War of
Independence
(1821–30) began, the
wealthy admirals of
Spétses and Ýdra turned
their guns on Turkish
targets. The Hydriot
captains under Andreas
Miaoulis (1769–1835)
sent flotillas of fire-ships
packed with gunpowder
which were sailed amid
the Turkish fleet, then
blown up. Spétses's most
famous daughter,
Lascarina Pinotzis
(1771–1825), nicknamed
Bouboulina, sailed at the
head of her own
squadron to raid Turkish
harbours and convoys.

from the harbour. Tel: (0297) 22637.
Open: Tue–Sun 8am–2.30pm.
Admission charge.

Palaiochóra

This derelict hillside village was Aígina's
capital until the 19th century and in its
18th-century heydays boasted around
400 houses and 20-odd churches and
chapels. Some of these, from as early as
the 13th century, have been restored.
Venetian ramparts crown the hill above.
8km east of Aígina Town, on the Agía
Marína road.

PÓROS

Tiny Póros is so close to the mainland
that you feel you could reach out and
touch it – at its closest the Peloponnese
is only 256m away.

The island has but one village, also
called Póros, and a scattering of shingle
beaches. This harbour village is on the
small peninsula of Sferia, facing the
mainland. A narrow isthmus, which is
known as Kalavria, connects Sferia to
the hilly, pine-wooded main body of
the island.
50km south of Peiraías.

Askeli

Askeli is Póros's best beach, and has
developed into a small but busy holiday
resort.
About 3km south of Póros Town.

Moní Zoodochos Pigi
(Monastery of the Source of Life)

This lovely whitewashed, cloistered
building is dedicated to the Virgin,
under one of her many Greek Orthodox
guises as the Source of Life. The
monastery stands in a grove of tall
cypresses and has splendid views of the
mainland coast. Below it, there is a
pleasant small beach for swimming.
4km east of Póros Town. Open: daily.
Admission charge.

The Temple of Aphaia, one of the best examples of island temples

Naós Possidhonia
(Temple of Poseidon)

The once great 6th-century BC temple has been reduced to a few stone walls and is worth visiting more for the location than for what is left of the structure. In the 18th century it was used as a quarry for marble blocks for the building of a monastery on Ýdra.

8km northeast of Póros Town.
Free admission.

Póros Town (Chóra)

Cheerful and busy, Póros Town and its white boxy houses cover a beehive-shaped hillock, which is connected by a bridge and causeway to the main part of the island. The streets on and behind the lagoon-like harbour are cluttered with colourful stalls and shops.

Boats shuttle to and from the harbour, taking visitors to beaches around the island or across the strait to the mainland.

West coast, on Sferia peninsula.

SPÉTSES

The furthest of the Argo-Saronic isles from Athens, Spétses is just off the southern tip of the Argolid peninsula. Much of the island is covered with pinewoods planted in the 19th century.

85km southwest of Peiraías.

Spétses Town

Numerous 18th- and 19th-century ship-owners' mansions are a feature of the island capital which is a hideaway for the many well-off Athenians who keep second homes here, giving Spétses a much more stylish air than most islands.

The hillside streets of Póros Town are home to colourful stalls and shops

The town is attractively laid out, with broad squares and avenues.
Northeast coast.

Ágios Nikólaos

The monastery of St Nicholas was the first building in the islands to fly the flag of independent Greece in 1821. Its courtyard is a mosaic of black and white pebbles in typically Spetsiot style.
On Palaio Limani (Old Harbour).
Open: daily.

Moussío Bouboulinas Laskarinas

The home of Spétses' famous female privateer (*see p48*).
Signposted from Palaio Limani. Tel: (0298) 72077. Open 9.30am–8.30pm.

Moussío Mexis (Mexis Mansion)

The former 18th-century home of Hadziyannis Mexis, one of Spétses' wealthiest merchants, is now a museum dedicated to the great Spetsiot admirals

of the 19th century, who played a leading role in the liberation struggle against the Turks.
Behind the Town Hall.
Open: 7am–2.30pm. Admission charge.

ÝDRA (Hydra)

Ýdra rides at anchor like a long, thin ship off the south coast of the Argolid peninsula. In the 18th century, at the height of its prosperity, Ýdra's merchant fleet numbered 160 ships, and 20,000 people lived here. The only vehicles on the island are two municipal trucks, and much of the island is covered by pines.
50km south of Peiraías.

Ýdra Town

Ýdra charms new arrivals with a steep façade of tall stone mansions, white houses with pantiled roofs, and a harbourside lined with chic cafés.
Midway along the north coast.

Arkhondiki

Many elegant 18th-century town houses belonging to the island's great merchant families have been preserved or restored, and some may be visited at certain times.
For visits, enquire at the Dhimotikon (town hall) on the waterfront.

Kamini

Ýdra's most accessible beaches are pebbly strands at Kamini and Kastello.
1,000 to 1,500m west of the harbour.

Mandráki

This is the only sandy beach on Ýdra and features a watersports centre.
3km east of the harbour.

Profítis Ilías and Agía Evpraxia

The monastery of Profítis Ilías and the nunnery of Agía Evpraxia face each other on a 500-m mountain slope. They are approximately two hours' steep walk from town, through young pine forests that have just begun to cover the scars of the forest fire of 1985.
2km south of Ýdra Town. Open: daily, except during prayer.

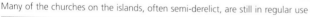

Many of the churches on the islands, often semi-derelict, are still in regular use

Kykládes
Cyclades

Lying in a scattered circle in the southwest Aegean, the many isles of the Cyclades archipelago are the archetypal Greek islands. Most are small and rocky, and some are no more than dots on the map, though Náxos, the largest of the group, is broad and fertile. Their white villages and blue-domed chapels are pictured on thousands of postcards, and most of them have at least one fine beach. It comes as no surprise, then, to find that the most popular of the group are among the busiest holiday islands in Greece, and that tourism has wrought dramatic changes. Islands which were peaceful and poor a generation ago are now lively holiday centres.

However, the most popular centres are still outnumbered by close neighbouring isles which see only a trickle of visitors each year. And, even on the busiest of islands, you can always find less visited spots.

Among the most popular islands are Mýkonos and Thíra (Santoríni), each with its own international airport; Páros, where ferry routes in all directions meet; and Íos, which has become Greece's most popular summer party island. Those less visited, except by Athenians and others in the know, include Folégandros, Sérifos, Síkinos, and Sífnos.

Before falling to the Turks in the mid-16th century, the Cyclades formed the Duchy of Náxos, ruled by the Venetian Sanudo dynasty who seized the islands following the Fourth Crusade in 1204.

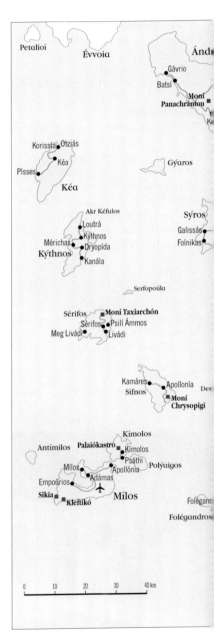

Cyclades

N

Sámos

Ikaría

Foúrnoi

ormos
Karkádos
Falatádos
s
Tínos
poli
Mýkonos
Mýkonos
Áno Méra
Platýs
Plíndir
Gialós
Paradíssi
Ríneia
Dílos
Pátmos

y k l á d e s

Náxos
Apóllon
Páros
Náousa
Náxos
Páros
Lat
Marmáron
Moutsoúna
aloúdes
771m
Pyrgos
Chalkí
Donoússa
ros
Velónia
1091m
Levítha
Chrysí
Náxos-Zéfs
pílaio
Alykí
Aktí
Kínaros
alaktitón
Alíko
Koufonísi
Órmos
Aigiális
822m
Amorgós
Schoinoússa
Kríkelo
Irákleia
Kéros
Moní Chozoviótissa
Amorgós
Katápola
Íos
Plakatos
Moní
Órmos Íou
Ágios Theodótis
chou Pigís
Íos
kinos
Mylopótamos
opi
Aloprónoia
Órmos
Astypálaia
Síkinos
Manganári
Ánydro
stásis
Astypálaia
Ofidoússa
Oía
Thíra
Thirasía
Thíra
(Santoríni)
Néa Kaméni
Kamári
Anáfi
Aspronísi
Arkhea Thíra
Akrotíri
Périssa

AMORGÓS

A slender, elongated island, peaceful Amorgós has a delightful hilltop capital (Chóra), uncrowded beaches, and a dazzling cliffside monastery. A sheer-sided mountain ridge connects the clusters of settlement and cultivation at either end of the island. Hilltops are often crowned by the round stone towers of medieval windmills, and cobbled hill-paths make Amorgós a fine island for walkers.

25km southeast of Náxos.

Amorgós Town

Amorgós's capital is a classic Cycladic village citadel of whitewashed lanes and archways around a flagstoned central square full of café tables. It sits on a ridge high above the shore with views north and south to neighbouring islands.

Approximately midway along the island's central ridge.

Kástro

The shell of the 13th-century castle of the Venetian Ghisi family crowns the village.

Signposted. Free admission.

Katápola

The western port is a sleepy harbour with a long waterfront which only comes to life with the arrival of the ferry.

4km below Amorgós Town, on the north coast.

Moní Chozoviótissa

The brilliant white walls of this 11th-century monastery cling miraculously to the bare cliff. Founded in 1088 by the Byzantine emperor, Alexios I Comnenos, its greatest treasure is a miracle-working, 11th-century icon of the Virgin, kept in its own gold- and silver-lined chapel.

3km northeast of Amorgós Town. Signposted. Open: daily 8am–2pm. Admission charge.

Órmos Aigiális

The island's eastern port sits on a tiny delta of fertile farmland beneath terraced slopes, rising to the bare 822m peak of Kríkelo. The small village has a long beach of sand and pebbles, and there are more secluded coves within walking distance to the east.

10km east of Amorgós Town, on the north coast.

ÁNDROS

Larger, more prosperous, and closer to the mainland than its Cycladic sisters, Ándros hardly seems one of the group at all. It has mostly resisted the temptations of tourism, though it has a couple of small resorts.

13km from the south coast of Évvoia, 35km northeast of Cape Sounion (Akr Soúnio).

Ándros Town (Chóra)

A modern harbour town, with two large beaches, plus some imposing 19th-century sea merchants' mansions.

On the east coast.

Moussío Arkheologiko (Archaeological Museum)

The highlight of the collection is the 4th-century BC statue of Hermes.

*Town centre. Open: Tue–Sun
8am–2.30pm. Admission charge.*

Batsí

Ándros's main resort has a fine sandy
beach, crowded in high season with
package holidaymakers and weekending
Athenians, lined with a modern strip of
hotels, bars, and tavernas.
12km west of Ándros Town.

Moní Panachrántou
(Panachrantos Monastery)

The 10th-century fortress monastery is
impressive but almost deserted, and
clings to grim, grey and red cliffs.
*4km southwest of Ándros Town.
Open: daily sunrise to sunset.*

ANTÍPAROS

See p66.

ASTYPÁLAIA

Geographically and culturally one of the
Cyclades, Astypálaia was lumped with
the Dodecanese islands (*see pp84–5*) by
an accident of history. When
international arbitrators were brokering
the independence of Greece from
Turkey (1832), they drew the line west
of the island, and it remained under
foreign rule until 1947.

The island is barren and rocky, almost
cut into two by deep bays. The isthmus
between them is just wide enough for
the road to pass. Though remote,
Astypálaia is popular with fashionable
Athenians and its only village, Astypálaia
Town, is surprisingly stylish.

Astypálaia Town (Chóra)

The chic island capital is striking even

The hillside monastery of Panachrántou has
wonderful views, but there are few monks to
enjoy them

by Cycladic standards. Its white houses,
with two or three storeys and pretty
painted shutters, combine influences
from its western sisters and from the
islands further east. They cover the
hilltop above a perfect natural
harbour.
Northwest Astypálaia.

Kástro

The dilapidated Venetian-Turkish castle
has an endearingly slapdash appearance.
Its walls are cobbled together from slabs
and blocks looted from earlier buildings.
It enjoys panoramic views to the empty
horizons around the island.
*On the highest point of the village.
Free admission.*

Dílos

See p60 & pp62–3.

FOLÉGANDROS

Tall and craggy, Folégandros looks like a stone ship steaming towards the mainland. Seemingly barren slopes, covered with terraces where barley and olives thrive, are testimony to centuries of hard peasant labour. The northeast coast of the island is dominated by sheer cliffs, while the more sheltered southwest side boasts a handful of small, undeveloped beaches.

The neighbouring isles of Thíra (Santoríni), Íos, and Síkinos can be seen on the horizon, and on a clear day islanders claim that they can see Crete, more than 100km to the south.
50km southwest of Náxos.

Folégandros Town (Chóra)

One of the loveliest Cycladic villages, Folégandros Town perches high above the sea among terraced hills and is built around the Piatsa, a flagstoned, central square. From the archway off the south side of the square, you enter the picturesque, dazzling white, fortress-like warren of archways and houses known as the Kástro.
In the centre of the island.

Khrissospilia

A startling blue sea cavern which bores into the cliffs of the north coast.
1km southeast of Folégandros Town, accessible only by boat from Karavostásis, the island's port, 3km southeast of Folégandros Town.

ÍOS

Greece's supreme party island throbs to a summer beat from June to the end of August, when it attracts young ravers from all over the world who pack its bars, beaches, and discos. It is quieter out of season, when it offers non-ravers a choice of fine, sandy beaches.
25km south of Náxos.

Ágios Theodotís

This long sandy stretch on the east coast of the island, overlooked by the ruins of a Venetian fort, is the less crowded of Íos's two easy-access beaches.
10km east of Íos Town.

Íos Town (Chóra)

Íos's Chóra conforms to Cycladic style, but dozens of bars, discos, and restaurants – virtually every building is now one or other of these – have obliterated the local culture.
On a hilltop on the island's west coast.

Órmos Íou (Yialos)

Íos Town's harbour annexe, immediately below the village, is on a fiord-like bay with its own beach where ferries call frequently.
1km west of Íos Town.

Mylopótamos

The closest beach to Íos Town and the most crowded despite its huge size, southwest-facing Mylopótamos is a solid mass of sunbathing bodies by day and beach slumberers by night.
1km from Íos Town.

Órmos Manganári

The least accessible of Íos's major beaches, Manganári's six small, silvery sandstrips face south and are reached by boat from Yialos.
12km southeast of Íos Town.

Plakatos ('Homer's Tomb')

Íos is one of many islands claiming a link with the author of the *Iliad* and the *Odyssey*. Be warned, however, that the remnants of the tomb at the site of ancient Plakatos are poorly signposted, difficult to reach, and are probably Byzantine.

Near the north tip of the island, 9km northeast of Íos Town. Free admission.

KÉA (Tzea)

Close to the mainland, Kéa is busy with Athenian weekenders in July and August but sees few foreigners and few visitors of any kind for much of the year. An egg-shaped isle with a hilly, wooded interior, it has little in common with its Cycladic neighbours.

20km east of Lávrio on the mainland, 90km northwest of Náxos.

Kéa Town (Ioulidha)

The main village, set in a pretty inland valley, is a mix of traditional red-tiled homes and newer buildings.

North central Kéa.

Arkheologiko Moussío (Archaeological Museum)

Collection of discoveries from four ancient Kéan sites.

Platía Mousiou. Open: Tue–Sun 8.30am–3pm. Admission charge.

Kástro

A tumbledown castle built by the Venetians, using remnants of an ancient sanctuary of Apollo.

1km from the village centre. Signposted. Free admission.

Lion of Kéa

This magnificent 3-m high stone lion was carved from the hillside in the 6th century BC.

2km northeast of the centre. Free admission.

A cluster of pristine white houses on the island of Íos

KÍMOLOS

This tiny satellite of Mílos is one of the Aegean's great undiscovered destinations.
1.5km from Mílos.

Kímolos Town (Chóra)

The island's main village is a clutter of white hillside houses backed by six windmills.
In the middle of the island, 1km from Psáthi.

Palaiókastro

The battlements of a ruined Venetian fortress surround the island's oldest church, the whitewashed Hristos chapel.
2km northwest of Kímolos Town. Free admission.

KÝTHNOS

Most visitors bypass gentle Kýthnos – the first stop on the ferry route from Peiraías to the western Cyclades – en route to better-known isles further south, and it is hard to argue that they are missing much.

Kýthnos has little to offer by way of beaches or sightseeing, and its landscapes are less dramatic than many of its neighbours.

Dryopída

Stucco-walled homes with red-tiled roofs make this farming village – the island's capital in medieval times – look more Italian than Cycladic.
5km south of Kýthnos Town.

Spíli Katafigi (Cave of Refuge)

In the middle of the village, the locally famous cave once provided islanders with shelter from pirate raids.
Free admission.

Kéfalos (Akr Kéfalos)

The ruins of a medieval Venetian castle crown the north-facing headland.
North tip of the island, 7km from Kýthnos Town. Free admission.

Kýthnos Town (Chóra)

The remaining traditional buildings of the village are dwarfed by new construction.
Centre of the island.

Metamórphosis (Church of the Transfiguration)

An interesting 17th-century church.
Village centre. Open: daily. Free admission.

MÍLOS

Mílos's weirdly sculpted landscapes are part of its appeal, not only for visitors but for the earliest Neolithic islanders, who valued the obsidian found in its volcanic soil. The island's soft rock is easily eroded by wind and water, and Mílos's coasts are marked by twisted stone formations and offshore islets carved by the sea. The island has also been shaped by human effort, and quarrying for cement and china clay continues today. Mílos is somewhat doughnut-shaped, with a wide, almost landlocked bay which takes a deep bite out of its north coast, and is less mountainous than most of the Cyclades.
161km south of Peiraías.

Adámas

Ferries call at the functional harbour

here on the east shore of the Gulf of Mílos.
5km from Mílos Town.

Mílos Town (Chóra)

The main island village is half-traditional, half-modern, with an assortment of sights, of which the ruins of the ancient city are the most worthwhile.
On the northern headland of the Gulf of Mílos.

Arkheologiko Moussío (Archaeological Museum) and ancient Mílos

Traces of the ancient city include the remains of the 5th-century BC acropolis, an intact Roman theatre, and 3rd-century AD Christian tombs. The archaeological museum collection includes Neolithic earthenware, and a replica of the *Venus de Milo*.
500km west/downhill from the village centre. Museum & site open: Tue–Sun 8am–2.30pm. Admission charge for both.

Kástro (Castle)

The small Venetian citadel is well preserved.
Hilltop site, 500m from village atop cobbled steps. Free admission.

Laografiko Moussío (Folklore Museum)

Costumes, furniture, and decorative items from everyday island life.
Village centre. Open: Tue–Sat 10am–1pm & 6–8pm. Admission charge.

Spília (Caves)

Mílos's volcanic shores have been hollowed out by the waves, and its coasts are pierced by several spectacular caverns, used in medieval times by piratical islanders. There are boat trips to the caves from Adámas.

Kleftikó (Robber's Caves)

White chalk cliffs and pinnacles, honeycombed with pirate caves.
South coast.

Papafranga (French Priest's Cave)

Three caves, big enough to shelter boats, tunnel into the cliffside.
South coast.

Sikia (Emerald Cave)

A trick of the light makes the water glow green here.
Near the southwest point of the island.

Souvenirs from Mílos: copies of the *Venus de Milo*

Superb sandy beaches, a stunningly attractive main town (for once at sea-level instead of high above) and, just offshore, one of classical Greece's most fascinating ancient temple sites make for a potent combination which attracts a very wide clientele. Wealthy Greek and expatriate villa owners rub shoulders with package holidaymakers (who fly direct to the island), cruise ship passengers who come ashore for a day's shopping and sightseeing, and a large gay community.

The first Aegean island to attract tourists in large numbers (more than 750,000 visitors a year), Mýkonos is the most popular and best-known of the Cyclades, with a worldwide reputation. Mýkonos nightlife is legendary and its holiday season is much longer than that of its neighbours, with a hard core of long-stay visitors who arrive early in the season and leave late. The island's famous beaches are strung along the south coast, sheltered from northerly winds, and conveniently accessible by a constant daytime shuttle of small boats.

Dílos, the finest ancient location in the Cyclades, is included in this section as it is most easily accessible from Mýkonos, but it has no accommodation. *25km north of Náxos.*

Dílos (Delos)

Dílos was sacred to the god Apollo and in the 5th century BC was the hub of the Delian League, a federation of islands dominated by Athens. Many of its temples were built during this era, others during the height of its prosperity as the most important

Whitewashed walls and narrow alleys are typical of Mýkonos

Aegean port in the early Roman era (2nd and 1st centuries BC). (For a full description of the site *see pp62–3.*) *10km southwest of Mýkonos Town.*

Arkheologiko Moussío (Archaeological Museum)

A fine collection of sculptures from the sanctuary of Artemis and the Temple of Athena, and smaller Hellenic finds of bronze, gold, and ivory.
Museum & site open: Tue–Sun 8.30am–3pm. Admission charge. Boats leave Mýkonos Town daily at 8.30am, returning around 1pm.

Mýkonos Town (Chóra)

Alefkandhra (Little Venice) is the most picturesque part of town, with brightly painted, wooden balconies suspended over the sea from the high white walls of Venetian town houses.
400m southwest of the harbour.

Arkheologiko Moussío (Archaeological Museum)

Decorated vases and other finds from sites on Dílos and the uninhabited islet of Ríneia.

South end of Andhronikou. Signposted. Open: Tue–Sun 8am–2.30pm. Admission charge.

Laografiko Moussío (Folk Museum)

A glimpse of old Mýkonos, a 19th-century island home with a traditionally decorated and furnished interior.

On the harbour, near Paraportiani church. Open: Mon–Sat 5.30–8.30pm, Sun 6.30–8.30pm. Free admission.

Mílos Boni (Boni Windmill)

The much-photographed, whitewashed, 16th-century windmill is one of the most evocative symbols of Mýkonos.

Leonidiou Boni, 300m east of the harbour. Open: Jul–Sep, daily 4–8pm.

Paradissi (Paradise Beach)

The most popular of Mýkonos's beaches, this sheltered bay is favoured by nude sunbathers.

6km southeast of Mýkonos Town.

Platýs Gialós

The closest to Mýkonos Town, and the most developed of the island's beaches, with lots of hotels. Platýs Gialós is on the sheltered west side of a south-facing bay, looking across to Psarou beach on the east shore.

4km south of Mýkonos Town.

Plindiri ('Super Paradise')

This is Mýkonos's best beach by far.

10km southeast of Mýkonos Town.

Vividly painted woodwork brightens Alefkandhra, nicknamed Little Venice

Cruise: To Dílos (Delos)

In ancient times, Dílos was a sacred and political centre and an important commercial port, and today its outstanding temple sites are among the most striking in Greece. The best way to visit them is by boat from Mýkonos. Boats depart daily around 8.30–9am, returning from Dílos at around 1pm.

The crossing takes approximately 30 minutes each way, leaving about 3 hours to explore the ruins.

Leaving Mýkonos harbour, you have a view of the balconies of Alefkandhra ('Little Venice') overhanging the sea. The boat turns south, passing through the narrows between Dílos and the neighbouring islet, Ríneia, before arriving at Dílos's harbour. There is a combined admission charge for site and museum.

At the landward end of the pier, turn north and enter the sanctuary district via the Sacred Way, where the bases of the statues which lined this wide access path can be seen. After 100m this leads to the three worn steps which are the remains of the Propylaia, the great gate.

1 Hieron (Sanctuary of Apollo)

To the left of the Propylaia are traces of the 6th-century BC *stoa* (covered walk) of the Naxiots; on the right are the rectangular foundations of the 7th-century BC temple known as the House of the Naxiots.

The heart of the sanctuary comprises traces of three temples of Apollo, around which are the column bases and foundations of three smaller religious buildings.

Walk 400m north, and leave the sanctuary via the walls of the 6th-century BC Temple of Leto, and the Agorá of the Italians on your right.

2 Lion District

The row of five stone lions sculpted in marble from Náxos during the 6th–7th

century BC are the best-known symbol of Dílos. Originally there were many more. To the east is the site of the Sacred Lake (drained in 1924 to prevent malaria) where swans dedicated to Apollo once swam.
Turn right, around the site of the lake, and head back south 350m to the museum, on your left.

3 Museum
The museum collection includes statues from the Sanctuary of Artemis, 5th-century classical art, Hellenic sculptures, and some delightful small bronze figures and ivory carvings.
Leaving the museum, continue south 500m to the lower slopes of Mount Kýnthos, Dílos's highest point. Allow 45 minutes for ascent and descent.

4 Mount Kýnthos (Óros Kýnthos)
At the foot of the hill is the Terrace of the Foreign Gods, where once stood statues of Syrian and Egyptian deities.
After 200m, pass on your right the Sacred Cave, a cleft in the rock which was sacred to Herakles (Hercules) and had massive granite doors.
Descending Mount Kýnthos, walk west 100m to the 2nd-century BC Theatre District.

5 Theatre District
On your right, the courtyard of the House of the Dolphins features a superb floor mosaic of dolphins, which were sacred to Apollo. Opposite, the restored two-storey House of the Masks is one of the highlights of Dílos, with more splendid mosaics. Finally, pass the well-preserved marble tiers of the Hellenic theatre, the House of the Trident, the House of Cleopatra (not connected with the famous Egyptian queen), and the beautiful panther mosaics of the House of Dionysos, before returning to the harbour.

The multi-tiered marble theatre seats date from the Hellenic era

NÁXOS

Varied landscapes and a rich trove of ancient and medieval finds make Náxos, the largest of the Cyclades, one of the most attractive islands in the group. Despite an air link to Athens, fine beaches, and a fascinating little capital, the impact of tourism is less visible here than on its nearest large neighbours, Páros and Mýkonos. There is room for more adventurous visitors to escape to empty beaches and a choppy landscape of farming valleys and high peaks.

Náxos is pear-shaped and measures some 35km from north to south. A steep ridge of peaks, rising to the 1001-m high Náxos-Zéfs, divides the barren and almost uninhabited east from the more populous and fertile west. Here, the coastal plain and inland pockets of rich soil are covered with lemon, orange, and olive groves, wheat, barley, and potato fields, and vineyards which produce some of the best wines in the islands.

Apóllon (Kouros of Apollo)

Apóllon is a quiet, pretty fishing village with a minute harbour and small beach. The reclining figure of a naked youth (*kouros*) was carved from the marble hillside some time in the 7th century BC, but for some reason was never finished. *Beside the ancient marble quarry, above the Chóra road, 33km northeast of Náxos Town. Free admission.*

Chalkí

A prosperous farming village set in the lovely pastoral landscape of the Tragéa valley, covered with lemon and olive groves, on the slopes of Náxos-Zéfs. *17km east of Náxos Town.*

Gateway of the 6th-century BC Temple of Apollo

Panayia Protothronos (Church of the Virgin)

Built over some 300 years of Byzantine rule (9th–13th centuries), the charming parish church has colourful frescoes. *Main street. Open: daily (if locked, enquire at community office on main street).*

Pýrgos Frangopoulo (Frangopoulos Tower)

A well-preserved mansion tower house. *Main street. Closed.*

Náxos Town (Chóra)

The island capital is a prosperous town. Its architecture blends Cyclades Cubism and faded medieval Venetian elegance. Courtyards filled with scented jasmine and crimson pelargoniums make its inner maze of alleys less austere than the whitewashed purity of Mýkonos or Thíra (Santoríni).

It became the capital of the medieval Duchy of Náxos in 1207 when the Venetian Marco Sanudo seized the island, and was ruled by his descendants for more than three centuries until its conquest by the Turkish pirate Barbarossa in 1566.

Arkheologiko Moussío (Archaeological Museum)

An outstanding collection of statues, Cycladic-era ceramics, and idols, well laid out and explained, housed in a 17th-century school.
Within the kástro. *Open: Tue–Sun 8am–2.30pm. Admission charge.*

Kástro (Castle of the Sanudos)

The pretty 13th-century castle is much less grim than its counterparts elsewhere. The ramparts are whitewashed and blend with the surrounding local houses, while the grand town houses within, built around inner courtyards, are still the private homes of Naxiot blue-bloods who claim descent from the Venetian nobility. Within the walls, too, are the Archaeological Museum and the Cathedral.
Village centre; follow Odós Apolonos uphill to main gate, flanked by a huge tower. Free admission.

Mitropoli (Cathedral)

The 13th-century cathedral, built by the first Sanudo, has a fine Byzantine icon of the Virgin and Ioannis Prodhromos (John the Baptist).

Within the kástro. *Open: daily. Free admission.*

Gateway of the Temple of Apollo

The towering marble gateway, all that remains of the grand 6th-century BC Temple of Apollo, is Náxos Town's most striking landmark. Locals believed it to be the portal of the palace of Ariadne, the lover of the legendary hero Theseus, abandoned by him on Náxos.
On Palatia headland, 500m north of the centre.

Pýrgos Velónia (Bellonia Tower)

This medieval tower house belonged to Roman Catholic bishops of the island.
6km southeast of Náxos Town. Not usually open to visitors.

The pristine façade of the church in Náxos Town

PÁROS

Páros has a good reputation, with excellent sandy beaches, an island capital which combines Cycladic charm with noisy summer nightlife, and a clutch of man-made and natural attractions. Two fine natural anchorages on the west and north coasts shelter the two main villages, and the roughly circular island rises to the 771-m peak of Profítis Ilías, summit of the Óros Márpissa massif which dominates the hinterland.

The satellite island of Antíparos is only minutes away by boat.

5km west of Náxos.

Antíparos

There are two reasons for a trip to Antíparos. First, the beaches – crowded in July and August – and second, its enormous limestone cave. The only village is on the north tip.

1km southwest of Páros.

Ágios Geórgios

This is the best and the most peaceful of the Antíparos beaches, a scattering of sandy coves facing southwest.

12km south of Antíparos village.

Spílaio Stalaktitón (Cave)

The great cavern is adorned with weirdly shaped rock formations and extends 90m into the hillside.

7km south of Antíparos village.
Signposted. Open: daily 9am–2pm.
Admission charge.

Chrysí Aktí (Golden Beach)

The best of Páros's sandy beaches, with smaller coves and beaches to either side.

15km southeast of Páros Town.

Gleaming chandeliers and wax tapers adorn the Church of Our Lady of the Hundred Doors

Latomia Marmáron (Marble Quarries)

Three ancient quarry tunnels, the earliest dating from Classical times, plunge deep into the hillside. Páros was famed for its pure white marble from ancient times into the mid-19th century, when the deposits were worked out.

6km east of Páros Town.

Náousa

The island's second-largest settlement, where a one-time fishing village has mushroomed into a medium-sized resort with small beaches to either side of a north-facing natural harbour.

On the island's north coast.

Pirgos (Tower)

A small stone keep of the Duchy of Náxos, built to guard the harbour.

On the harbour. Free admission.

Páros Town (Chóra)

Páros, the island capital, has one of the busiest harbours in the Cyclades, with ferries calling constantly day and night. Its 1.5-km esplanade is lined with cafés, bars, and restaurants, which at night would seem to compete to generate the brightest lights and the loudest music.

Arkheologiko Moussío (Archaeological Museum)

This small collection includes pottery and marble fragments and a 6th-century BC statue of Athena Nike.
Next to Panagia Ekatotapyliani. Open: Tue–Sun 8am–2.30pm. Admission charge.

Kástro (Castle)

This ruined 13th-century Venetian castle incorporates columns and marble blocks from an ancient temple which stood on the same site.
Northern promontory of the bay, 1km from Páros Town centre.

Panagia Ekatotapyliani (Katapoliani/Our Lady of the Hundred Doors)

The original Byzantine church dates from the 6th century, with some 10th-century additions. Its chapel of Ágios Nikólaos incorporates columns from an earlier Hellenistic temple.
Off Manto Mavrogenous. Open: daily 8am–noon & 5–8pm. Free admission.

Petaloúdes (Valley of the Butterflies)

The Valley of the Butterflies is undoubtedly the island's most charming and colourful attraction. Lemon and apricot trees are grown on both sides of the valley, sheltering vast swarms of scarlet-winged tiger moths which take to the air in an explosion of colour. Visit in spring or early summer for the best display.
7km south of Páros Town. Open: daily, daylight hours. Admission charge.

Náousa is a cheerful blend of fishing village and holiday resort

Oía, reborn as a holiday village

THÍRA (Santoríni)

The view of Thíra (Santoríni) from a ferry pulling into its cliff-ringed bay is unforgettable. Sheer cliffs in layers of red, white, and greenish-grey volcanic rock encircle a huge, sea-filled *caldera* (crater) which plunges to an enormous depth and is encircled by Thíra (Santoríni) and its smaller neighbours, Thirasía and Aspronísi. It also has two tiny, still-active volcanic islets that smoulder gently in the centre of the *caldera.*

Shaped like a broken circle, the island was formed by a huge volcanic explosion (c.1450 BC) which blew out its centre, leaving the present huge *caldera.* Many archaeologists believe the explosion and the enormous tidal wave it created may have been the nemesis of the Crete-based Minoan civilisation which collapsed at about the same time. (Minoan and Mycenaean sites have also been excavated on Santoríni.) In more recent times, the island was also an important medieval possession of the Dukes of Náxos.

Santoríni's main town, Thíra, is a line of white battlements along the crater rim. South of it, the rolling hills rise a little further to the walls of Pýrgos, a half-deserted fortress-village. To the east, the island shelves seaward in a series of terraced tomato fields and vineyards before reaching the sea at the black-sand beaches, Kamári and Périssa, on Santoríni's east coast. A crescent ridge running from Pýrgos to the east coast divides the island into two, and an ancient city (Akrotíri) once sat atop its seaward end.
50km south of Náxos.

Akrotíri
(Akrotíri Archaeological Site)

The well-preserved houses and streets of this 'Greek Pompeii', smothered by the great eruption, have been excavated since 1935, unearthing graceful 3,500-year-old frescoes which demonstrate the connection with the Minoan civilisation. Some minor finds from the site are displayed in the Thíra Archaeological Museum.
South coast of the southern cape, 18km south of Thíra. Tel: (0286) 81366. Open: Tue–Sun, summer 8am–5pm; winter 8.30am–3pm. Admission charge.

Kamári

Santoríni's biggest resort is on a long, east-facing beach of black sand which becomes uncomfortably hot in the summer sun.
12km southeast of Thíra.

Arkhea Thíra (Ancient Thíra)

Scant remains possibly dating from a 6th century BC–5th century AD settlement include foundations of an ancient *agora* and a theatre.

On top of the Mesavouno headland, 2km south of Kamári and 320m above it. Open: Tue–Sat 8am–2.30pm. Admission charge.

Oía

This dazzlingly pretty clifftop village commands huge views, both across the northern and western horizon, and south to Thíra and Akrotíri. It was badly shaken by a minor eruption and tremors in 1956, and remained almost deserted until its restoration in the 1980s.

Many of its houses have typical Thíra (Santoríni) barrel-vaulted roofs (to withstand earth tremors), and some have rooms burrowed deep into the soft volcanic rock. A few have been converted into characterful guesthouses (*see p177*).

There is a small beach immediately below the village, reached by a steep stair cut into the rock.
8km north of Thíra.

Thíra Town (Chóra)

Thíra's geometric buildings form a whitewashed parapet atop 270-m high sea-cliffs. Visitors arriving by sea reach the clifftop town either by donkey, up some 600 breathtaking steps, or by a dizzying cable-car ride from the harbour.

There are tiny blue-domed churches at every corner, but these are outnumbered by fast-food cafés and expensive jewellers. Thíra is just too photogenic to have escaped mass-market tourism, and like Mýkonos (*pp60–61*) has been welcoming visitors since the early 1960s.

Arkheologiko Moussío (Archaeological Museum)

A fine collection spanning two millennia, from the Minoan era to the Roman period.
Ipapantis St. Open: Tue–Sun 8am–2.30pm. Admission charge.

Multicoloured cliffs of soft volcanic rock loom over Thíra's harbour

Looking over the huge, sea-filled crater of Thíra (Santoríni), you can see two jagged black islets in its centre. These are the Kaméni, the 'burnt islands', and you can visit them on a boat excursion from the main island.

Palaia Kaméni, the older of the pair, has been there since the 2nd century BC, when it astonished the Greek world by emerging from the sea in a matter of weeks – proving to the ancients the power of Poseidon, god of the sea and of earthquakes.

Néa Kaméni, the bigger of the two, made its appearance over AD 1707–11. It trebled in size during another eruption in 1866–7, and still shows some signs of activity, with a reek of sulphur from a pool of hot, bubbling mud.

It may be because of this whiff of brimstone that the Kaméni and Thíra (Santoríni) are said to be haunted by vampires – not the Dracula variety but the less substantial Greek kind: wandering spirits which moan and wail at night and are also said to inhabit the deserted hills and canyons of Sfakiá, in southwest Crete. The garlands of wildflowers that islanders gather on 1 May and hang above their doors for the rest of the year bring blessings on the home and keep such evil spirits from crossing the threshold.

While all craters look awesome, some are more forbidding than others – an evil stench of brimstone hangs over the Néa Kaméni crater (left)

Many archaeologists now believe that the explosion which blew the island apart some 3,500 years ago may also have destroyed the thriving Minoan civilisation which dominated the Aegean at that time.

With its capital at Knosós on Crete, the Minoan empire included colonies on Thíra (Santoríni) and other Cycladic islands, but around the time of the Thíra eruption, it collapsed suddenly and inexplicably. The eruption, it is now believed, would have sent huge waves in all directions, destroying ports and cities throughout the Aegean and smothering crops and fields under centimetres of poisonous ash.

As a comparison, when the Indonesian island of Krakatoa (Krakatau) exploded in 1883, it raised 15- to 30-m high tidal waves, and damaged buildings more than 160km away. It is thought that the Thíra explosion was even bigger than Krakatoa, and as Knosós, on Crete, is only half that distance from Santoríni, the damage to the city, its surrounding lands, and to other Minoan settlements would have been extensive.

This 'big bang' theory may not wholly account for the disappearance of the powerful Minoan empire from the Aegean stage, but the timing is persuasive. By the 15th century BC, the Minoans were no longer a great power, and Mycenaean settlers from the mainland had moved in to take over the islands they once controlled.

Cruise: Thíra (Santoríni) Crater

This cruise gives superb views of the fantastically coloured volcanic cliffs of Thíra (Santoríni), with the white villages of Thíra and Oía clinging to the rim of the giant sea-filled crater – the most striking island landscape in the Aegean. Tickets for the trip are sold by tour agencies in Thíra and Kamári, and at the larger resort hotels (if you are on a package tour they can be booked through your tour representative).

Boats depart from Skála Thíras, at the foot of Santoríni's west-coast cliffs, directly below Thíra. Most departures are at 9 or 9.30am, returning mid-afternoon.

1 Donkey Ride

A cobbled, zig-zag staircase descends for 270m from just below Thíra to the small pier at Skála Thíras. You will have to haggle furiously over the price if the donkey ride is not included in the price of your excursion. Of course, you could simply walk down.

The walls of Thíra's vast crater are banded with colours

2 Crater Wall

Leaving Skála Thíras, look back for a magnificent view of the multicoloured, 270-m high cliffs, banded with shades of red, pink, white, and green volcanic rock. Fragments of porous pumice stone can be seen floating in the bay.
After 15 to 20 minutes, land at Néa Kaméni, 2km west of Athiniós.

3 Néa Kaméni

The eerie, lifeless island of shattered black rock is the product of a series of volcanic eruptions (*see pp70–71*). Hot springs and boiling mud trickle from cracks in the rock and a smell of sulphur hangs over the islet. Just south and west of Néa Kaméni is the smaller Palaia Kaméni, also formed by volcanic activity in the 2nd century BC.
The boat sails round Néa Kaméni's north coast, heading west towards Thirasía. Look south for a view of Santoríni's dramatic southern cape, Akrotíri, where archaeologists have unearthed remains of a Minoan settlement almost 3,500 years old (see p68).

4 Thirasía

Thirasía is a tinier reflection of Santoríni. Its cliffs are all that remain of the original island, shattered by a titanic explosion 3,500 years ago. As on Thíra, the main village – also called Chóra – is reached by steep steps from the harbour below. Pause here to enjoy the view across the crater. Chóra has several small, scenically located tavernas which will allow you to do just that while enjoying a cold drink.

Walk west and downhill across the island (30–45 minutes each way) to a choice of small, pebbly, and sandy coves on its western coast, where you can swim and sunbathe; or take the less energetic option, and swim from the tiny pier below Chóra, where the deep blue water is extremely clear and shoals of colourful fish make for excellent snorkelling.

5 Oía

On the return boat trip, look north to the clifftop village of Oía, perched on the extreme tip of Santoríni. It was shaken badly by tremors in 1956, but is now restored to pristine whiteness. Below the village at sea level, you can see the mouths of tunnels carved into the soft volcanic rock, used by the islanders as homes, stables, and boathouses.

6 Cable-Car Ascent

From Skála Thíras, take the dizzying cable-car ride from sea level to the cable-car station for a final view of Thirasía and the crater islands.

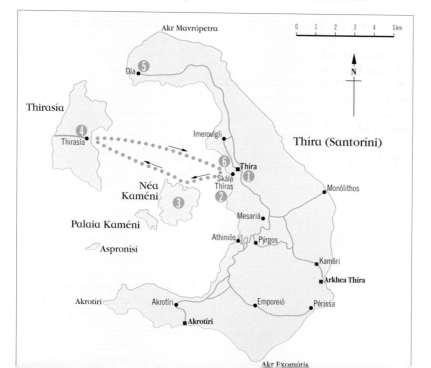

SÉRIFOS

Sérifos is how many people picture all the Greek islands. White houses, churches, and a miniature castle all cling precariously to a crag some 2km inland from a perfect natural harbour on a shallow sandy bay. Around the bay, square houses splashed with purple and scarlet flowers clutter the hillside, where clumps of greenery cling to the scree and boulder-strewn slopes of rocky ravines.

131km southeast of Peiraías.

Livádi

Sérifos's port is a cheerful, house-proud assortment of mostly modern, well-kept homes, tavernas, and small hotels, enhanced by its bayside location and mountain backdrop. A tiny fertile delta of green farmland and pink oleander-lined creeks stretches behind the village. The tree-lined beach south of the village is not the island's best: there are much better, small sandy beaches 10 to 30 minutes' walk away, beyond the headland west of the harbour.

2km southeast of Sérifos Town.

Mega Livádi

The west-facing beach is the remotest and least-visited large beach on the island.

8km southwest of Sérifos Town.

Moní Taxiarchón (Monastery of the Archangel Michael)

The 16th-century monastery is often deserted, with a single guardian monk sporadically in residence. There are some minor frescoes within, but the visit is worth making as much for the

Sérifos Town on its inland hilltop overlooks Livádi harbour

walk through serene hill landscapes as for the destination.

2km northwest of Kállitsos village, 5km north of Sérifos Town. Access on foot from Kállitsos. Sketchily signposted.
Open: irregular hours. Enquire at Sérifos Town community office or at Kállitsos.

Psilí Ámmos

Sérifos's best beach, with a lovely crescent of white sand facing east.
4km north of Livádi. Access on foot or by boat.

Sérifos Town (Chóra)

Sérifos Town is built around and within the walls of a Venetian castle, which is virtually absorbed into the buildings around it. Unlike some Chóras, therefore, it does not stand in splendid isolation, but is just another part of the pleasant jumble of old stones and whitewashed walls.

2km from the east coast.

SÍFNOS

The island of Sífnos, rising steeply from the sea, is patchworked with fields and pastureland, criss-crossed with donkey-tracks marked out by drystone walls, and dotted with white hill-villages.
136km south of Peiraías.

Apollonía (Chóra)

Three characterful hamlets – Artemón, Kamáres, and Kataváti, originally about 750m from each other – have blended into a single jumble of whitewashed houses, church towers, and small café-cluttered squares.
Centre of the island.

Ágios Spiridon (Church of St Spiridon)

The island's main church, built and added to over several centuries, is a fine example of the Sifniot taste for multi-coloured religious architecture, painted in gaudy shades.
On Stylianou Prokhou, the main street.

Laografiko Moussío (Folk Museum)

Beautiful island lace and embroidery, displays of traditional Sifniot costume, and a rusting collection of lethal weaponry.
On the central square at Kamáres.

Open: daily 10am–1pm & 6–9pm. Admission charge.

Kástro

This medieval Venetian stronghold occupies the finest natural fortress on Sífnos, a sea-crag guarded on three sides. Its distinct alleys, archways, and two-storey houses suggest a strong Venetian flavour.
East coast, 4km east of Apollonía.

Arkheologiko Moussío (Archaeological Museum)

Small collection of finds from the ancient site.
Pano Kástro. 3km east of Apollonía, on the coast. Open: Tue–Sun 8am–2.30pm. Admission charge.

Moní Chrysopigí (Chrissopiyi Monastery)

The picturesque 17th-century monastery, located on a promontory on the east coast, is one of the island's tourism symbols. It is decon-secrated, and you can stay in one of the monks' cells in summer.
6km southeast of Apollonía.
Tel: (0284) 31225.
Open: sunset to sunrise.

Apollonía church tower is a blend of Greek and Italianate styles

SÍKINOS

Tiny, rocky Síkinos is for Greek island purists. It has a high fortress-village, a port with a small beach, a few other small beaches around its rocky coasts, and two minor sights.
25km southwest of Náxos.

Aloprónoia (Skala)

The port of call for inter-island ferries and yachts; also boasts a small beach.
Southeast coast.

Episkopí ('Temple of Apollo')

A Hellenic building, perhaps a temple or mausoleum, transformed into a church in the 7th century.
5km southwest of the kástro (castle).

Moní Zoodóchou Pigís
(Monastery of the Spring of Life)

A deserted monastery with fine views over the island and its neighbours.
750m above the kástro.

Síkinos Town (Chóra)

Two medieval villages on the rocky spine of the island have merged into one, around a square of fortified medieval houses.
4km from Aloprónoia.

SÝROS

One of the most populous islands, with 20,000 inhabitants, Sýros is fertile on its west side, barren on its eastern coast, and blessed with the southern Aegean's finest deep-water anchorage.
40km northwest of Náxos.

Ermoúpoli

Ermoúpoli, Sýros's capital, is no dinky village but a thriving town of 15,000 folk. Its grandiose town architecture and Neo-Classical public buildings date from the first half of the 19th century, when it was newly independent Greece's most prosperous city. What's more, it wasn't until the completion of the Corinth Canal in 1893 that it was eclipsed by Peiraías, the port of Athens.

The lower part of the town, between the harbour and main square, Platia Miaoulis, was laid out in the island's heyday. Above it, on two hills, Áno Sýros to the west and Vrondado to the east, are the town's contrasting medieval quarters. Áno Sýros is a labyrinthine collection of alleys and arches with a scattering of Catholic churches dating from the Venetian era, while Vrondado is the town's Orthodox quarter.

Anastasi

The grand, domed Orthodox church was built to rival neighbouring Ágios Geórgios.
At top of Vrondado, 1km north of Platía Miaoulis. Open: irregular hours. Enquire at town tourist office, Platía Vardhaka.

Arkheologiko Moussío
(Archaeological Museum)

Finds from Sýros and nearby islands.
West side of the town hall. Signposted. Open: Tue–Sun 8.30am–3pm. Admission charge.

Ágios Geórgios
(Cathedral of St George)

The Roman Catholic cathedral is built in the Venetian style.
On top of Áno Sýros, 1km from Platía Miaoulis. Open: daily. Free admission.

Moní Kapoutsino
(Capuchin Monastery of St John)
Built in 1535, the monastery survived the Turkish era under French protection.
100m downhill from Ágios Geórgios. Open: daily. Free admission.

Foínikas/Poseidonía
Sýros's main beach resort, where two villages at either end of a pebble-and-sand bay which faces west have merged.
11km southwest of Ermoúpoli.

TÍNOS
Tínos is the contemporary national shrine of the Greek Orthodox religion. Its tradition as the 'Lourdes of the Aegean' began in 1822, when a sacred icon was revealed in a dream to the nun later beatified as Agía Pelagía. The island is also renowned for its picturesque, geometrically patterned dovecotes, which date from Venetian times.
65km northwest of Náxos.

Tínos Town (Chóra)
Modern and unassuming, the town's main attraction is the famous, imposing white-marble Church of the Annunciation housing a sacred icon.
Southwest coast.

Arkheologiko Moussío
(Archaeological Museum)
This is housed within the church complex, and displays discoveries from sites on the island, notably an enormous 7th-century BC *pithos* (storage jar).
Leoforos Megalochoris. Open: Tue–Sun 8am–2.30pm. Admission charge.

Panagía Evangelistría
(Church of the Annunciation)
Built in 1822 to house a newly discovered icon with its healing powers, this huge, fortress-like church complex is the venue for two annual pilgrimages, on 25 March and 15 August.
Leoforos Megalochoris. Open: daily 8.30am–8.30pm. Free admission.

The church of St Nicholas overlooks the busy harbour at Ermoúpoli

Kríti

Crete

Crete is Greece's biggest island – more than 200km long from its western to its eastern tip. It's really a country within a country, with its own history, folklore, and traditions. Only a very concise description of this most magnetic of islands is possible within this book: for a comprehensive guide to the island see *Thomas Cook Travellers Crete.*

A yacht-filled harbour welcomes tourists

Most of the hundreds of thousands who come to Crete each summer stay in the large resorts on the north coast. The south coast of the island is generally less developed: resorts and hotels are smaller and, except in high season, beaches are less crowded.

Inland, Crete is one of the most rewarding islands to explore, with soaring mountain ranges, remote hill-villages, and hidden, oasis-like valleys, lush with orange and lemon groves. Its major towns are rewarding, too, but in a different way. Crete was one of the jewels of Venice's Aegean empire, and from their mighty fortresses at Irakleío,

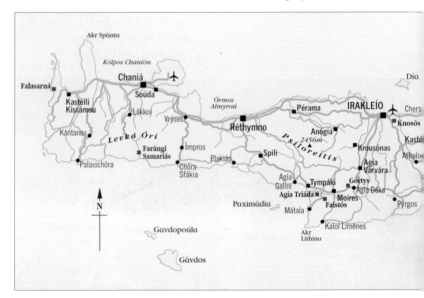

Réthymno, and Chaniá, the Venetians held the island they called Candia until finally driven out by the Turks in 1669. Cretans rebelled repeatedly against the Turkish yoke and finally achieved *enosis* (union) with Greece in 1913.

From the late third millennium BC, Crete was the seat of the Minoan empire – Europe's first civilisation – which controlled much of the Aegean from elaborate palaces such as Knosós and Faistós. After the collapse of the Minoan world around 1500 BC (*see pp70–71*), the island's importance faded until Roman times. As Rome's power dimmed, Crete was ravaged by barbarian pirates, then in AD 823–4 it was seized by Arab invaders from Andalusía. The great Byzantine commander Nikiforos Fokas recovered Crete in 961; then in 1204, it was seized from the crumbling Byzantine empire by the Venetian Republic.

Snow-capped White Mountains overlook the little town of Chaniá

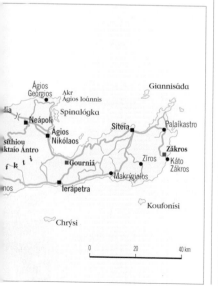

Crete is long and thin, lying east to west, and is the southernmost of the main Greek islands. For this reason spring comes early, in a blaze of wildflowers, and in summer, which lasts longer than on any other Greek island, it can really be extremely hot.

As well as its treasury of ancient and medieval history, Crete has breathtaking mountain scenery and wonderful beaches. On the north coast, Mália and Chersónisos are large-scale holiday resorts with long sandy beaches. Ágios Geórgios (Georgioupolis), also on the north coast, has a long stretch of fine sand too, but is not quite so built-up. On the south coast, the best sandy beach is at Mátala, with shingle and pebble beaches at Plakiás, Agía Galíni, and along the southwest coast.

The 16th-century Venetian fortress guards the harbour at Irakleío

Chaniá (Khania)

A pretty, old-fashioned town with pastel-coloured Neo-Classical mansions around a harbour overlooked by Venetian walls. Immediately behind the harbour esplanade is an old quarter of narrow alleys and overhanging balconies weighed down with pots of flowers and herbs.

127km west of Irakleío.

Arkheologiko Moussío (Archaeological Museum)

Mysterious Minoan relics, Hellenic marbles, and Roman pottery and jewellery are on display here.

Halidhon is signposted. 100m from the harbour. Tel: (0821) 20334. Open: Tue–Fri 8am–4.30pm. Admission charge.

Faistós (Phaestos)

Hilltop remains of a Minoan palace dating from c.2200 to 1700 BC.

56km southwest of Irakleío. Tel: (0892) 22615. Open: weekdays 8am–5pm, weekends 8am–6pm. Closed: public holidays. Admission charge.

Górtys

Splendid ruins of a Hellenic-Roman city with an early Christian basilica, temple foundations, and *agora*.

44km south of Irakleío. Tel: (081) 226092. Open: daily 8.30am–3pm. Admission charge.

Irakleío (Iraklion)

Crete's capital and main port is mainly commercial, but a visit to its excellent museum and the colourful palace site at Knosós is essential.

Midway along the north coast.

Arkheologiko Moussío (Archaeological Museum)

Here you can see magnificent frescoes from Knosós, Minoan seals and ornaments, statues, and other finds from Hellenic and Roman sites.

Just off Platía Eleftherias. Signposted. Tel: (081) 226092. Open: Tue–Fri, except public holidays. Free admission.

Arsenali (Venetian Arsenal)

The great archways of the Venetian Arsenal (shipyard), now used for storing boats and fishing gear, overlook the old harbour.

Close to the foot of 25 Avgoustou. Free admission.

Koulos (Harbour Fortress)

The 16th-century castle guards the Venetian harbour. Its walls seem capable of resisting any bombardment.

At end of pier; access from junction of Venizelou and 25 Avgoustou. Tel: (081) 246211. Open: Tue–Sun 8.30am–3pm. Admission charge.

Porta Khanion (Chaniá Gate)

Massive 17th-century Venetian ramparts ring the town centre and are easiest to see at Porta Khanion, where the main

road passes through the old gateway at
the junction of 62 Martiron and
Plastira. Bastions can also be seen at the
eastern end of the walls at the junction
of Makariou and Venizelou, and at the
western end at the junction of Venizelou
and Doukous Bofor.

Knosós
The most imaginatively reconstructed
palace site in Greece, with colourful
columns, halls, and avenues of the
millennia-old palace.
*5km southeast of Irakleío. Tel: (081)
231940. Open: daily 8am–5pm. Closed:
public holidays. Admission charge. Bus 2
from city bus terminal, on Epimenidhou.*

Lasíthiou
The verdant 'Plain of Windmills', ringed
by bare 1,000m-plus peaks, is still a joy,
though most of the windmills are long
gone and water is drawn to the fertile
fields of this mountain oasis by petrol-
driven pumps.
61km southeast of Irakleío.

Diktaío Spília (Dhikti Cave)
In this green, mossy 250-m deep cavern
full of twisted stalagmites, Zeus,
king of the ancient gods,
was born – or so legend
has it. Less disputable are
the relics that have been
found, indicating that
people worshipped here
from Neolithic to Roman
times.
*1km above Psychró village
car park. Signposted. Steep
path, mule hire available,
torch recommended for*

cave. Tel: (0834) 31207. Open: Jul–Sep
sunrise–sunset. Admission charge.

Réthymno (Rethimnon)
The lanes and cobbled market streets
of this old harbour town are overlooked
by a mighty fortress, and the older part
of town, with its fountains, ramparts,
palm trees, and abandoned minarets,
combines Turkish, Venetian, and Neo-
Classical influences.
95km west of Irakleío.

Arkheologiko Moussío (Archaeological Museum)
Coins from all eras are the centrepiece
of a collection which also comprises
sculpture, bronzes, and jewellery.
*Off Melissinou, opposite the southwest
corner of the castle walls. Tel: (0831)
29975. Open: Tue–Sun, summer
8.30am–3pm; winter 8am–2.30pm.
Admission charge.*

Jami Nerandzi (Nerandzi Mosque)
Enjoy an overview of the harbour, old
quarter, and castle from the top of this
slender Turkish survival.
*West end of Mesolongiou. Minaret open:
daily 11am–7pm. Free admission.*

Kástro (Castle)
This is the largest Venetian
castle ever to have been built,
and dates from the late 16th
century. Today, its interior
is a ghost town of barracks,
churches, and storerooms.
*Open: daily sunrise–sunset.
Free admission.*

Detail on Irakleío's fortress

Walk: Faràngi Samariàs

Samaria Gorge

This challenging but very rewarding walk takes you through the most impressive mountain scenery in the Greek islands, from the top of the longest mountain gorge in Europe to the lovely pebble beach at Agía Rouméli. The gorge is a national park, so camping, swimming in the freshwater pools, and straying from the marked track are prohibited. It is open from May to mid-October, depending on rainfall.

Allow 4 to 6 hours for this strenuous 18km walk.

Start from Omalós village, 36km south of Chaniá. The head of the gorge is signposted Xylóskalo. On leaving the village, you will receive a numbered ticket (no admission charge) which you surrender at the other end.

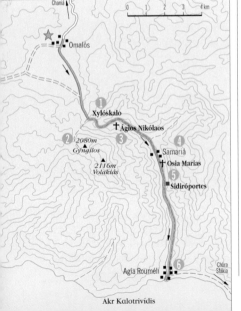

1 Xylóskalo (Wooden Stair)

The wooden steps, made of solid logs, start at 1,227m above sea level and drop steeply into the bottom of the gorge, turning into a footpath which descends almost 1,000m along a 2km stretch.

2 Gýngilos

Above you on your right, as you start the descent, is the towering flank of Mount Gýngilos, climbing to a sharp peak almost 1,000m above Omalós. *After the steep descent, the path becomes less tiring and zig-zags down grassy slopes, amid pine woods, with springs gurgling in the rocky stream bed.*

3 Ágios Nikólaos

The tiny, whitewashed chapel of Ágios Nikólaos, with candles always burning in front of its icons, stands in a small pine wood to the right of the path. *1½–2 hours' walking from Ágios Nikólaos, through pine forest and across the stream bed, will bring you to the deserted village of Samariá.*

4 Samariá

This ghost village, with its derelict stone cottages and abandoned mill and olive press, has been deserted for half a century. One house is used as the park warden's office. Samariá is the midway point of the walk, and there is an official picnic area under the pines where you can take a break.

From Samariá, the path passes another small chapel, Osia Marias, then winds along the stream bed, crossing it several times by chains of water-smoothed boulders. The gorge narrows like a funnel, with the slopes on either side becoming steeper until you reach the narrowest point.

5 Sidiróportes (Iron Gates)

The gorge is narrowest at this point. Grey cliff walls, marked with the rust-coloured stains of iron-bearing springs, shoot vertically to 600m. High above, the sky is a narrow strip of blue. Water surging through the narrows makes the gorge impassable in winter and early spring, and even in summer you may have to take off your shoes and paddle across the stream.

From Sidiróportes the gorge fans out into a boulder-filled delta, and the cliff walls recede to become steep, rocky slopes, wooded in places. Walking is fairly easy for the final 5km to the sea at Agía Rouméli.

6 Agía Rouméli

This tiny village exists only to service the steady flow of summer walkers. A chain of tavernas and small guesthouses extends the length of a pebbly beach ending in cliffs to the west but extending several kilometres eastward. The water is very clear and a swim is welcome.

Independent travellers can opt to stay overnight at Agía Rouméli before walking on eastward to Chóra Sfákia (where the road from Chaniá ends), or to travel on east or west by boat. Those on organised tours will be transferred by boat to Chóra Sfákia to meet their coach.

Xylóskalo, the wooden stair, drops steeply into the Samaria Gorge

Dodekánisos

Dodecanese

The Dodecanese island group contains something for everyone, with an array of landscapes ranging from the farmlands of Ródos (Rhodes) and Kós to the stark hillsides of Kálymnos and the smouldering volcanic crater of Nísyros.

Little to disturb the natural beauty of this island

There are big, bright beach resorts, miniature havens that see only one ferry a week, mosques and monasteries, ancient temples and medieval castles. The chain of islands runs close to the Turkish coast in Greece's southeast Aegean, and the name 'Dodekánisos' means 'twelve islands' – but the Dodecanese also includes an assortment of tiny isles whose people are numbered only in hundreds or even in dozens. These include Megísti, Greece's easternmost outpost, within a few hundred metres of Turkey; Saría; Psérimos; and the mini-archipelago of Leipsoí (Lipsi), Arkoí (Arki), and Agathónisi (Agathonisi), east of Pátmos.

Some of these, such as Psérimos and Leipsoí, are close to popular vacation islands and are regularly invaded by flocks of day-trippers. Others, such as Agathónisi or Arkoí, attract only the most determined of island-hopping solitude-seekers. Isolation and seclusion are their main attractions, and facilities for tourists (where they exist at all) are usually modest (*see pp150–55*).

With frequent ferry and hydrofoil connections between the major islands and to Peiraías and other island groups

north and west, the Dodecanese group is perfect for island-hopping.

Man-made sights include the grand walled city of Rhodes, restored to its medieval splendour, the fortified monastery of St John on Pátmos, and the ruins of classical, Hellenic, and Roman cities on Kós and Rhodes.

Dodecanese houses have a distinctive style of their own, typified by tall two- and three-storey homes with Neo-Classical stucco façades in pastel shades, tall doors, and shuttered windows. Many have wooden or wrought-iron balconies poised precariously above the street, and most have gardens or courtyards overflowing with vines, pelargoniums, and often banana and palm trees. You will also see elaborate Art Deco public buildings, erected during the Italian occupation (1912–43).

The climate is mellower than that of the windswept islands of the central Aegean. The Dodecanese are spared the gusty *meltemi* which sometimes plagues the Cyclades, and Rhodes claims more hours of sunshine per year than anywhere else in Europe, making it the only truly year-round holiday destination in the Greek islands.

Dodecanese

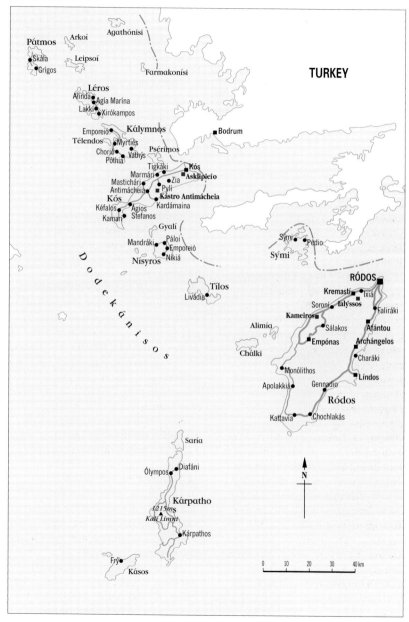

Pátmos
Arkoí
Agathónisi
Skála
Grígos
Leipsoí
Farmakonísi

TURKEY

Léros
Alinda
Agía Marína
Lakkí
Xirókampos

Emporeió
Télendos
Myrtiès
Kálymnos
Chorió
Váthys
Psérimos
Póthia

Bodrum

Tigkáki
Marmári
Mastichári
Antimácheia
Kós
Kéfalos
Kamári
Agios
Stefanos
Zia
Pyli
Kós
Asklipieío
Kástro Antimácheia
Kardámaina

Gyalí

Mandráki
Páloi
Emporeió
Nisyros
Nikiá

Symi
Pédio
Sými

RÓDOS
Kremastí
Ixiá
Soroní
Ialýssos
Faliráki
Kameiros
Sálakos
Afántou
Empónas
Archángelos
Charáki
Monólithos
Líndos
Apolakkiá
Gennadio
Ródos
Kattavia
Chochlakás

Tílos
Livádia

Alimía

Chálki

D o d e k á n i s o s

Saría

Ólympos
Diafáni

Kárpatho
1215m
Kali Límni

Kárpathos

Frý
Kásos

N

0   10   20   30   40 km

The arms of the Knights of St John on the castle

KÁLYMNOS

Kálymnos is an island of deep blue, fiord-like bays and striking bare white limestone hills, pockmarked with caves and dotted with green valley deltas of cultivation where the mountains meet the sea.

With so little fertile land, islanders have (until the advent of tourism) been dependent on the sea, and Kálymnos's sponge-divers ventured as far as the North African coast, Florida, and even Cuba. These days, the sponges which are sold everywhere on the island are more likely to have been imported (many, ironically, from Florida) than to have been hauled up by local divers.
15km north of Kós.

Chorió

Chorió is Kálymnos's medieval capital, built inland for protection from pirate raids. It is now a residential hillside suburb of Póthia, with many dignified old homes in tree-filled gardens.
3km northwest of Póthia.

Kástro

The small, crumbling castle is Byzantine, more than 1,000 years old, with Venetian additions dating from the 13th century. The heraldic arms of the Knights of St John are carved above the gateway.
200m above the village. Free admission.

Emporeió

From its pebbly beach, this tiny fishing hamlet (just waking up to the possibilities of tourism) seems to be entirely landlocked, with steep hillsides rising to surround a deep, calm, crystal-clear inlet which offers fine swimming and snorkelling.
16km northwest of Póthia.

Masourion and Myrtiés (Mirties)

These two fishing hamlets lie at either end of a stretch of beach on a bay which is sheltered by the long, thin islet of Télendos. They have grown into a pleasant small resort strip of small hotels, pensions, and restaurants. The beaches are a mix of pebbles and sand and the water is calm and very clear.
8–9km northwest of Póthia.

Póthia

Prosperous from the 19th-century sponge trade, Póthia is a charmingly cluttered harbour surrounded by dolls' house-like mansions and cafés, patronised by elderly traders and captains in panama hats or seamen's caps, many of them retired from sponge-fishing in Florida or the Bahamas.
On the south coast.

Dhimotikon (Town Hall)

The town hall is a fine example of the 'Art Deco Moorish' style invented by the Italians for their public buildings in the Dodecanese, with elaborate domes,

arches, round windows, and plaster mouldings.
Midway along the harbour front.

Moussío Vouvalis (Vouvalis Museum)

An imposing and lavishly furnished mansion, once the home of Nikolaos Vouvalis, father of the island's sponge industry. He had offices in London and a business empire which stretched from Kálymnos across the Saronic islands, as far as North Africa, Nassau, and Tarpon Springs, Florida.
Signposted. Open: Mon–Fri 8am–2.30pm, weekends 8.30am–1pm. Admission charge.

Palaiókastro (Knights' Castle)

A crest of the Knights can be seen above the castle gateway. The ruined walls enclose a small Orthodox Chapel of the Panagía (Virgin).
2km northwest of Póthia. Free admission.

Rina

Rina is the miniature port of the farming settlement of Vathys. It is an enchanting ex-pirates' lair, where a narrow arm of the sea, only barely wide enough to allow fishing boats or yachts to pass, widens into an inner lagoon. The cliffs shelter the inlet and the village, and radiate the sun's heat in summer, even after sundown. Swim from the steps at the end of the pier, which lead into deep, clean water.
6km northeast of Póthia.

Télendos

Télendos, Kálymnos's tiny and mountainous satellite, shelters the waters off Myrtiés and Masourion, and has beaches and a little hamlet of its own. There are regular small boats from Myrtiés that run throughout the day in summer.
1km west of Myrtiés.

Barren hills rise behind Póthia, the sleepy harbour capital of Kálymnos

KÁRPATHOS

Kárpathos is a lonely island. Long sea crossings separate it from its nearest large neighbours, Crete in the southwest and Rhodes in the northeast. Rugged and mountainous, it has excellent beaches and attractive villages. A charter airport ensures that, despite its remoteness by sea, it gets its share of tourism, but as Kárpathos is the second largest of the Dodecanese (after Rhodes), it absorbs its summer visitors without becoming overcrowded.

An island of changing landscapes, its fertile southern half is connected to the more barren and mountainous north by a knife-edged mountain ridge which in places is just wide enough to carry the road. Bus rides can be vertigo-inducing. In the north is one of the island's highest peaks, Profítis Ilías, reaching 1,140m.

Like many islands, Kárpathos lost many of its people to emigration in the 19th and early 20th centuries, most of them heading for the eastern United States, which is why you may meet older men, retired to their island birthplace, speaking fluent English with Brooklyn and New Jersey accents. Many family homes have been colourfully rebuilt with money earned overseas. Local tastes run to vivid blue and green plasterwork, domes and archways, offset by purple and crimson bougainvillea.

Though Kárpathos shares some of the history of its Dodecanese neighbours to the east, with occupation by Byzantines, Venetians, Knights of St John, and Turks, none of them left much in the way of tangible remains, but Kárpathos compensates for that by offering walkers the finest rambles in the Dodecanese, whether in the gentler valleys and vineyards of the south, or in the breathtaking mountain landscapes of the north.
60km southwest of Rhodes.

Amopi

Kárpathos's growing holiday resort has a choice of three sandy beaches and an increasing number of hotels and tourist tavernas.
8km south of Pigádia (Kárpathos Town).

Ólympos

The principal village in northern Kárpathos, Ólympos is awesomely situated on a high, windy ridge which plunges sheer to the west coast of the island. A line of stone windmills stands along the ridge, some of them still in use. Above the village is the peak of Profítis Ilías, the island's highest point. Ólympos was one of the most isolated villages in the Aegean until the building of the road from Pigádia in 1980. Its small port, Diafáni, 3km away on the east coast, is too small for inter-island ferries to dock. As a result, it retains much of the old-fashioned self-sufficiency and many of its traditions, including the local costumes worn by village women (*see p144*).
40km north of Pigádia.

Pigádia (Kárpathos Town)

The capital is a well-kept, unassuming modern harbour where boats call en route from Rhodes to Crete. Its redeeming feature is its proximity to the fine, 2km sandy beach of Órmos Vrondis, which begins immediately

north of the harbour.
On the southwest coast.

Vroukounda (Vrychonta)
These scattered ruins of various eras include the foundations of a small temple, a Byzantine-Turkish keep, rock graves, and a shrine to Áyios Ioannis Theológos (St John the Divine) in a cliff cave.
North of Pigádia. Free admission.

KÁSOS
This southernmost island of the Dodecanese group is a delight for island purists. Here tourism has had zero impact. There are no sights to see and nothing to do except ramble among tiny fields and olive groves, sit in cafés and tavernas, and swim and sunbathe.
10km south of Kárpathos.

Frý
The island capital is ringed by mountains and set on a rocky bay, enlivened only by infrequent ferries from Crete and Kárpathos. Its dignified older homes belong to ship-owning families whose fleets brought some prosperity to the island in the 19th century, and its port, Emporeió, is a 10-minute walk away.

A line of dilapidated windmills stands on the ridge above Ólympos on Kárpathos

KÓS

Kós, the third largest of the Dodecanese, is a long, fish-shaped island of changing landscapes. The higher slopes of Mount Dikios (Óros Díkeos), which dominates the northeast of the island, are rugged and treeless, while its lower slopes are clad with pine and fig-trees.

Northwestern Kós is covered by wheat fields and cattle pasture. Inland, much of the island is a plateau of meadows, thorn-trees, and goat pastures. The southern tip is mountainous, but its shores are studded with small beaches.

There are excellent beaches all over Kós, and the island is a favourite holiday destination for northern Europeans.

Like Rhodes, Kós was a stronghold of the Knights of St John, who left behind two formidable castles. Turkish and Italian occupiers also left their mark.

In 1933, the island was struck by an earthquake which levelled much of Kós Town, allowing the Italian authorities to excavate archaeological sites that had been built over.

Midway up the chain of the Dodecanese, Kós has excellent connections by ferry and hydrofoil to its neighbours, and westwards to the Cyclades and Athens, making it a popular island-hopping junction.

Kálymnos, Psérimos, and Nísyros are all close enough to be popular day-trip destinations, as is Bodrum in Turkey.
110km northwest of Rhodes.

Kardámaina

Kós's biggest and busiest resort features long, southeast-facing beaches to either side of a small fishing harbour, surrounded by a long strip of bars, discos, hotels, and restaurants. Until the late 1970s, it was no more than a village. Today it could be anywhere in Greece. The conical silhouette of the isle of Nísyros (*see pp96–7*) can be seen on the southern horizon, and excursion boats arrive daily from Kardámaina harbour in summer.
25km southwest of Kós Town.

Kástro Antimácheia (Antimachia Castle)

The impressive angular battlements surrounding the hilltop date from the mid-14th century. The Knights of St John rebuilt the castle in the 15th century, and the crest of Grand Master del Caretto is carved above the main gate (which itself is within a much later Italian gun-casement). The small chapel of Agía Paraskevi within the ramparts dates from 1494.
18km southwest of Kós Town, 4km northeast of Kardámaina. Free admission.

Kéfalos

Kéfalos is a small, relaxed resort overlooking one of the island's best beaches, the long, south-facing strip of Kamári. It is the best place on Kós for a quieter holiday, avoiding the crowds and the frenzied nightlife of Kardámaina. There are other beaches to the north and south, reached on foot over hill paths, or by small boats which operate frequently throughout the summer.
45km southwest of Kós Town.

Ágios Stefanos (Basilica of St Stephen)

Ruins comprising the walls and columns of a 5th-century Christian basilica.

North end of Kamári Bay, next to the Club Méditerranée resort. Free admission.

Palatia (Ancient Kós)
A 4th-century BC sanctuary of Demeter and the tiered seats of an ancient theatre have been excavated at the site of the island's first city. In 366 BC, the capital of the island was moved to the site of modern Kós Town.
2km southeast of Kéfalos. Free admission.

Kós Town (Chóra)
The modern capital is an agreeable blend of Greek and Roman ruins, medieval fortifications, Turkish leftovers, and florid Italian public buildings. Visitors can mingle with the everyday bustle around the crescent harbour and the busy market area, where high-piled produce stalls, gaudy souvenir stores, and smart goldsmiths' shops stand next to each other.
East end of the island.

Agorá
The site of the *agorá* (Hellenic marketplace), dating from the 4th century BC, contains foundations of several temples, sections of the town walls, a Christian basilica, and the extensive foundations of the Roman city of Kós.
Access from Platía Eleftherias. Signposted. Tel: (0242) 28763. Open: Tue–Sun 8am–2.30pm. Admission charge.

Beach umbrellas line Paradise Beach, one of the prettiest on Kós

Palm trees and bougainvillea brighten the ruins of the Castle of the Knights

Arkheologiko Moussío (Archaeological Museum)

The main exhibits are the 4th-century BC statue of Hippokrates and a mosaic of Asklipios (see Asklipieío). Other finds span the 3rd century BC to the 2nd century AD.

Platia Eleftherias. Tel: (0242) 28326. Open: Tue–Sun 8am–2.30pm. Admission charge.

Asklipieío

This is one of the best preserved and most beautifully located sacred places in the Aegean islands. Seven white Corinthian columns of a 2nd-century AD Roman temple have been re-erected, and the arched walls of the terrace have been rebuilt. Two columns of the 4th-century BC Temple of Asklipios (god of healing) can also be seen.

4km southwest of town centre. Signposted. Tel: (0242) 28763. Open: Tue–Sun 8am–2.30pm. Admission charge.

Casa Romana

A reconstruction of a 3rd-century AD Roman villa with mosaics, three inner courtyards, and baths.

Grigorioutou Pemptou. Tel: (0242) 28326 Open: Tue–Sun 8am–2.30pm. Admission charge.

Kástro

The medieval Knights' castle, a low square of sloping ramparts and turreted bastions that stands guard over the harbour.

South side of harbour. Open: Tue–Sun 8am–2.30pm. Admission charge.

Odeion

The *odeion* (Roman theatre) has 14 tiers of marble seats. Opposite, on the other side of Grigorioutou Pemptou, is a second extensive archaeological site, covered with a confusing clutter of marble capitals and fallen columns.
West end of Grigorioutou Pemptou.
Open: Tue–Sun 8am–2.30pm.
Admission charge.

Marmári

Kós's west coast is an almost continuous strip of sandy beaches, but prevailing strong winds make them less popular among holidaymakers than the more sheltered strands of the southeast. There are exceptions, and Marmári is one of them. Windsurfers rate it among the best in Europe for its steady breezes.
Southwest coast, 15km southwest of Kós Town.

Mastichári

An unassuming port with a small beach, Mastichári's main attraction is the ferries which leave regularly for Kálymnos and the little island of Psérimos. Southwest of Mastichári, the coast is windswept and unappealing.
West coast, 30km southwest of Kós Town.

Pylí

The ruined ghost village of old Pylí on the southwest shoulder of Óros Díkeos (Mount Dikeos) is appealing in a tumbledown way. Hidden in a wooded glen, it is surmounted by the shell of a Byzantine tower. Half a dozen small chapels indicate that the village was quite prosperous in its medieval heyday, when its inhabitants huddled below the protecting castle to escape marauders from the sea. Unfortunately, their wall-paintings are not well preserved.
1km southeast of modern Pylí, 23km southwest of Kós Town.

Tigkáki

The best beach close to Kós Town. Tigkáki is sandy, but like all the west coast beaches it can be blustery.
12km west of Kós Town.

Zia

Zia is the most visited and the prettiest of the Mount Dikeos villages. By night, tour coaches arrive for typical 'Greek evenings' in recently built tavernas. Come here in the daytime for the fine mountain scenery and the views of the island and of its northern neighbours.
12km southwest of Kós Town.

Fast hydrofoils link Kós with its Dodecanese neighbours to north and south

LÉROS

Léros is a peaceful island which sees far fewer visitors than its neighbours to the north and south. Its beaches, if not breathtaking, are certainly uncrowded, and its harbour towns, if not over-endowed with purpose-built tourist attractions and facilities, are undeniable slices of authentic Greek island life.

There is also a fertile hinterland of rolling hills, terraced fields, and olive groves, which is ideal if you like undemanding rambles in a rural setting. This is one island where the locals still outnumber the visitors all year round.

Léros's coastline is deeply indented, making it look like a piece from a jigsaw puzzle, and though it is only 17km from its northern to its southern tip it has more than 70km of coastline. The superb anchorage at Lakkí, on the west coast, made the island a strategic prize in World War II. The events on which the book and film *The Guns of Navarone* are loosely based took place here in 1943 when, following the Italian capitulation, British troops attempted to occupy the island before it could be secured by Germany, only to be expelled by a stronger and better-supported German force. The islanders and their homes suffered severely in the fierce fighting.

Agía Marína (Platanos)

Agía Marína, Léros's eastern port, is really three villages which have merged into one higgledy-piggledy town spanning a hilly, castle-topped headland with harbours on either side. Agía Marína surrounds the main northern harbour; Pandeli lies on a smaller fishing harbour; Platanos, below the castle on the headland, separates Pandeli and Agía Marína.

East coast.

Kástro (Platanos Castle)

The first castle on this site was built by the Byzantines, but the tower and ramparts which now crown the village were strengthened by the Venetians and the Knights of St John, and are again being restored. The castle is still garrisoned by the Greek army, as its location, with panoramic views over many kilometres, makes it a perfect lookout point.

Within the castle is a small museum exhibiting pottery and other finds from excavations around the island, and a small monastery church, Panayía (Church of the Virgin). No monks live here any more, but there is a reputedly miraculous icon of the Virgin.

Immediately above centre of Platanos. Signposted from Platanos. Open: sunrise–sunset. Free admission. Photography forbidden. Church open: irregular hours.

An unusual combination of two familiar images

Bright yellow nets at Agía Marína, Léros's main harbour

Alinda

The best beach on the island and its only developed resort, Alinda has a narrow, shingly beach, and attractive views across the bay to the castle at Agía Marína (Platanos), Léros's only historic sight.
4km northwest of Agía Marína.

Lakkí

Lakkí, on one of the finest natural harbours in the eastern Mediterranean, is a near ghost town with the languid atmosphere of a deserted film set. Grandiose public buildings and an open-air cinema behind a crumbling Art-Deco façade (the style chosen by the Italians for their Aegean possessions) are dotted about a grid of wide, dusty boulevards, lined with palm and eucalyptus trees. It has an unfinished look, perhaps not surprisingly, as Italy's Aegean adventure, which began with the seizure of the Dodecanese from Turkey in 1912, ended ignominiously in 1943.
West coast, 4km south of Agía Marína.

Xirókampos

The northern coast of the neighbouring isle of Kálymnos, not far south of Lakki, appears almost to fit into the narrow bay of Xirókampos, where a small farming village sits among fields and palm trees behind a long, narrow beach.
10km south of Agía Marína.

NÍSYROS

The tiny southern neighbour of Kós, Nísyros is blessed with a charm out of all proportion to its size.

Its conical slopes surround a vast inner hollow, in the very centre of which a crater of sulphurous mud bubbles alarmingly. By contrast, picturesque white villages cling to the rim of the crater, looking outward over thickly wooded slopes.

The island's volcanic soil is extremely fertile, and this, together with earnings from the cement quarries on the islet of Gyalí, has given Nísyros a degree of peaceful prosperity.

Seen from a distance, the thick bush clinging to its slopes makes the island look almost tropical, though its beaches don't live up to this first impression, comprising pebbles and brownish sand. As a result, Nísyros sees few tourists apart from excursionists from Kós, who make a flying visit to the crater before heading back, and it still feels pleasantly remote from 'civilisation'.
12km south of Kós.

Emporeió

This almost deserted village has one small café among tumbledown houses, and spectacular views out to sea and the Kós coast. For equally awesome views down into the old crater with its patchwork of fields, follow the whitewashed steps to the highest point of the village, where there is a pretty hilltop church in good repair.
6km east of Mandráki.

Krateir (Crater)

Around the crater, the hillsides are

Blue-painted balconies in Mandráki's main street

streaked with sulphur, and the air smells like the aftermath of a fireworks display. The crater itself is a bowl 250m wide and 30m deep. Fumaroles emit steam from deep underground, and grey mud, stained by brimstone-yellow sulphur deposits, heaves, and bubbles. Here at the bottom, the ground temperature can reach 120°C.

Nearby, an EU-funded project aims to harness the crater's geothermal energy.
Centre of the island.

Mandráki

Most of the island's 900 or so inhabitants live here in the main village, a network of narrow lanes and squares rising uphill from the esplanade, where fish tavernas sit by the sea wall. These look north to Kós and the strange silhouette of the quarry island Gyalí. The harbour, where ferries and excursion boats from Kós dock, is about 750m east of the village.
Northwest corner of the island.

Historiko kai Laografiko Moussío (Historical and Ethnographical Museum)

A restored village home with traditional interiors and furnishings.

*Signposted between village centre and
Panagía Spiliani. Open: irregular hours.
Admission charge.*

Palaiókastro

Grim ramparts of spectacular black
volcanic rock guard the island's oldest
defensive site. It has been fortified
throughout the ages, from the Dorian
era (2,600 years ago) to the days of the
Venetians and the Knights of St John.
*1km south of the village. Signposted.
Free admission.*

Panagia Spiliani (Church of the
Virgin of the Cave)

Built into the mountain, within
battlements erected by the Knights of St
John, this monastery church dates from
1600, and has a valuable iconostasis.
*Overlooking the village. Signposted.
Open: daily sunrise–sunset.
Admission charge.*

Nikiá

This spectacularly located village makes
a dazzling splash of white against the
rugged mountainscape of the crater rim.
10km southeast of Mandráki.

Moní Ágios Ioannis Theológos
(Monastery of St John)

A whitewashed monastery church,
perched precariously on the upper
slopes, looking down into the crater.
*500m below Nikiá, on the signposted path
to the crater. Not usually open.*

Páloi

This little fishing village has a large
harbour where traditional wooden
fishing boats are built and yachts
anchor, plus an esplanade lined with
tamarisk trees. To the east, its long
brownish sandy beach is the most easily
accessible on Nísyros.
3km east of Mandráki.

The brilliant white village of Emporeió perches above the volcano

PÁTMOS

Pátmos is an island of great natural and man-made beauty, crowned by the ramparts of an impressive medieval monastery and by the most striking village in the Dodecanese.

On the coast, lovely blue bays almost cut Pátmos in two and there are lots of secluded little beaches. Inland, low rocky hills are covered with terraced fields, divided by a maze of drystone walls topped with thorns. Ranks of eucalyptus trees, a late introduction, shade island streets, and fig trees, bougainvillea, and prickly pear cluster around houses and villages.

The fact that Pátmos has been proclaimed a holy island, maintains monastic conservatism, and has no airport, has helped to keep tourism quite low-key, though the legendary monastery does make this one of the better-known islands in the Dodecanese.

60km northwest of Kós.

Grígos

Pátmos's most accessible beach lies in a steep-sided east coast bay. The setting is hard to beat, though the beach is pebbly and no better than average.

5km south of Skála.

Pátmos Town (Chóra)

The hilltop village of Pátmos Town is one of the most beautiful in Greece, well worth the steep walk up from Skála. Tall mansions in grey stone and white plaster date from its 17th-century heyday, when islanders owned a substantial merchant fleet. Around them are simpler village homes. The colours are austere, an almost monochrome mix of white walls and grey stone doorways and arches, and it is almost impossible to keep a sense of direction in these corridor-like lanes, stairs, and passages. Pátmos Town – like many old Greek villages – is much bigger than it appears at first sight. To find your way out of the maze, just keep heading downhill.

1–2km above Skála.

Moní Ágios Ioannis Theológos (Monastery of St John the Divine)

The grand monastery around which Chóra is built is Pátmos's claim to fame. Founded in the 11th century, it was self-governing under the Byzantine emperors and kept its independence when the Venetian Dukes of Náxos acquired Pátmos in the 13th century. Its grim black battlements and bastions make it look more like a fortress than a place of worship. They were built to

Gorgeous mosaics decorate the Monastery of St John the Divine

Deep blue bays, almost cutting Pátmos in two, make Skála a perfect anchorage

protect the treasures of the monastery from pirate raids and were added to throughout the Middle Ages, with the great sloping buttresses dating from the 16th century.

Inside the walls is a central courtyard lined with domed arcades and paved with a mosaic of black pebbles. The Katholikon (main church) of the monastery stands to the left of this courtyard. Built in 1090, its interior is decorated with 17th-century frescoes of the life of St John. The chapel of the Virgin in the main church has remarkable late 12th-century frescoes, uncovered and restored in 1958.

Next to the Katholikon is the monastery museum, which has a gorgeous collection of icons, holy vestments, and church furniture.

Centre of the village. Signposted.

Open: daily 8am–noon, 3–6pm (afternoon hours may vary). Admission charge.

Skála

The island's main village and harbour is on a perfect anchorage, which makes it a popular port of call for yachts. It is a verdant, flower-filled village, and its handful of medium-sized hotels are unobtrusive among the more traditional whitewashed buildings. The harbourside is lined with café tables which, after dark, attract a more stylish clientele than you would expect on this remote little island, many of them Athenians and foreigners who own homes in Pátmos Town.

The grand black battlements of the Monastery of St John frown down on Skála from their hilltop site.

East coast.

The Knights of St John

Founded to succour wounded Crusaders and pilgrims in the Holy Land, the Knights of St John were expelled from Palestine after the fall of Acre in 1291, and settled on Cyprus until they transferred to Rhodes in 1309. Seizing the Dodecanese as well as the port of Bodrum on the Turkish coast, they built new castles or strengthened existing fortifications on almost all the islands. They also built a city of palaces and lodges – one for each of the 'tongues' of the order – within the great ramparts of Rhodes.

Each 'tongue' represented one of the eight different lands – Aragon, Auvergne, Castile, England, France, Germany, Italy, and Provence – whose lodges and crests you can see on Odós Ippóton, the restored Street of the Knights in the old town of Rhodes.

There were never more than 650 Knights of the order in total, though with their wealth they commanded a fighting force of much greater numbers.

The Knights ruled the seas of the Eastern Aegean for the next two centuries, and though they claimed to be defenders of Christendom their galleys preyed on any vessels they could catch, including those of Greek islanders and merchants. In 1522, however, Suleiman the Magnificent attacked Rhodes with a huge fleet and a 100,000-strong army. Only 200 Knights survived the six-month siege, finally withdrawing after

a negotiated surrender. As they were vastly outnumbered, it was a tribute to their fighting prowess and to the strength of their defences that they held out so long. The huge stone cannonballs fired by the Turkish siege guns can still be seen littering the dry moat around the old quarter.

The Knights later moved to Malta, granted to them in 1530 by the Holy Roman Emperor Charles V. Though their piratical ways did not endear them to their Greek neighbours, Mussolini decided that they were suitably militant role models for Fascist Italy, and under the Italian occupation of Rhodes the battlemented Palace of the Grand Masters, the lodges of the eight 'tongues', and other relics of the Knights were painstakingly restored, which explains why they are in such good repair compared with most other medieval buildings in the Greek Islands.

The Knights' strongholds: Castle of the Knights of St John at Líndos (above); the walls of Rhodes Old Town (bottom); detail in the Street of the Knights in Rhodes (above left)

Ródos (Rhodes)

The biggest and most important island of the Dodecanese chain, Rhodes has some of Greece's best beaches, a fascinatingly intact medieval city, more sunshine than any other Greek island, and, in Líndos, the most picturesque of island village resorts as well as the most luxurious and modern 5-star hotels in Greece.

A touch of the east and classical Roman

The eponymous capital of the island is really two towns rolled into one. The restored medieval quarter, within the 14th-century ring of walls built by the Knights of St John, is an eye-catching mix of historic buildings, museums, colourful shopping streets, and unchanged old-fashioned homes and workshops in narrow alleys. Plentiful palm trees plus mosques and minarets (a few still used by the city's handful of Muslims) give the old quarter a distinctly eastern flavour.

In classical times, the island was divided between three powerful city states – Ialýssos, Líndos, and Kameíros – which banded together in 408 BC to build a new capital, Rhodes, on the site of today's city. Remnants of the ancient capital can be seen on the slopes of Monte Smith, and at a newly discovered site on Odós Panetiou.

The new town, built around the Mandráki harbour, is a more commonplace blend of homes, shops, hotels, restaurants, bars, and discos

Bronze deer, the emblem of Rhodes, stand guard over Mandráki harbour

Rhodes

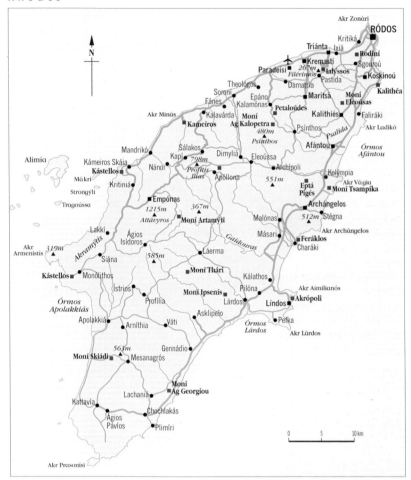

behind a rather grand waterfront of pompous Italianate public buildings and arcaded cafés.

Large holiday resorts spread either side of Rhodes Town on both the east and west coasts, and Líndos is the hub of a second concentration of resort beaches. The west coast, often windswept where it is not mountainous,

is less visited, and inland, especially in the south, is a different world of rolling hills and farms.

Rhodes's smaller satellites, the islands of Sými, Chálki, and Tílos, are within easy reach by hydrofoil, fast catamaran, or ferry, and a small fleet of excursion vessels sets out each morning from Mandráki harbour.

Afántou

Popular Afántou, with its long shingle
beach, is less crowded than other beaches
nearer Rhodes Town and is somewhat
less built-up. Small pebbly coves at
either end offer potential privacy.
22km south of Rhodes Town.

Charáki

An unexploited fishing hamlet, Charáki
has an excellent empty sweep of clean,
pebbly beach beside its little harbour.
The shell of a small castle of the
Knights, on a low hill at its north end,
adds a touch of historic colour.
East coast, 40km south of Rhodes Town.

Faliráki

The island's biggest and noisiest resort
appeals to an international clientele in
search of watersports, beach life, and a
vivacious after-dark scene. The beach,
long and of coarse sand, with an
excellent choice of watersports, is the
main attraction and is crowded for
almost the whole season.
East coast, 12km south of Rhodes Town.

The ancient acropolis and 15th-century fortress
above Líndos

Ialyssos (Ancient Ialysos)

Foundations of a 3rd-century BC Temple
of Athene and Zeus, and a particularly
fine example of a Doric well-house from
300 BC are highlights of this site.
15km southwest of Rhodes Town.
Tel: (0241) 21954. Open: Tue–Sun
8am–2.30pm. Admission charge.

Ixiá

The first resort outside Rhodes Town
on the west coast is fast turning into a
virtual suburb of the city. Most of the
island's international luxury-class
hotels, with amenities such as
landscaped grounds and swimming
pools, are located here – just as well,
since the beach here is long but narrow
and gritty.
West coast, 3–4km south of Rhodes Town.

Kameíros

The graceful columns and foundations
of the ancient city of Kameíros are
located within walls constructed later
in medieval times. They have been
excavated and partly restored by Italian
archaeologists.
35km southwest of Rhodes Town.
Signposted from main coast road.
Tel: (0241) 21954. Open: Tue–Sun
8am–2.30pm. Admission charge.

Líndos

The prettiest village on Rhodes and one
of the most charming in Greece, Líndos
is noted for its unique homes, built
around courtyards with elaborate
mosaics in black and white pebbles.
Traffic is banned in the village centre,
and the little village is completely taken
over by tourism.

Graceful 3rd-century BC columns mark the site of the Temple of Apollo on Monte Smith

Acropolis

The Acropolis of Líndos is built on a 180-m high sea cliff, protected by impregnable 15th-century battlements. The Gothic gate and stair and a partially ruined church of St John stand among the ruins of the 5th-century BC temple precinct ruins. High points are the 2nd-century BC 'Ship of Líndos', a relief of a galley carved into the rock by the main gate, and on the highest point the columns of the 4th-century BC Doric Temple of Athene.

Within the walls of the castle, immediately above the village. Signposted. Tel: (0241) 21954. Open: Tue–Sun 8am–2.30pm. Admission charge.

Monólithos Castle

This ghostly, abandoned 15th-century castle was built by the Knights on a pine-covered crag to watch over the southern part of the west coast.

83km southwest of Rhodes Town. Signposted. Free admission.

Monte Smith (Ágios Stefanos)

Three slender 3rd-century BC columns on the hillside mark the site of the Temple of Apollo and the ancient acropolis of Rhodes. Below them is the restored 3rd-century BC stadium and *odeion* (theatre).

1km southwest of Rhodes Town. Tel: (0241) 21954. Open: 8am–2.30pm. Free admission.

Petaloúdes (Valley of the Butterflies)

Despite the valley's popular name, the colourful scarlet-winged insects which swarm here in July and August are in fact tiger moths. Outside the moth season, when no coach parties visit the valley, it is a pleasant green retreat.

26km southwest of Rhodes Town. Open: 8am–sunset. Admission charge.

Walk: Rhodes Old Town

This walk takes in the best features of the picturesque old quarter, with a look at ancient relics, medieval fortifications, and Turkish survivals. High points include the various Inns (headquarters and lodgings) of the 'tongues' of the Knights, and the restored Palace of the Grand Masters.

Allow 2½ hours, plus half an hour for the Archaeological Museum and time for shopping on Odós Sokrátous.

Rhodes Old Town is a labyrinth of alleys

1 Píli Navarhíou

Enter the Old Town by Píli Navarhíou (Admiral's Gate), off the south end of Mandráki harbour. An arched stone bridge crosses the dry moat, where a small herd of deer – once the sacred animal of the city – is kept.

Pass through the arched gateway which pierces the massive walls to enter Platía Alexándrou.

2 Pand Auvergne (Inn of the Auvergne)

The arched doorway of the 14th-century inn leads into a courtyard with a fountain made of marble blocks taken from early Byzantine churches. The Inn of the Auvergne is on the east side of the square. On the west is the 14th-century Arsenal (armoury) of the Knights, now the Museum of Decorative Arts.

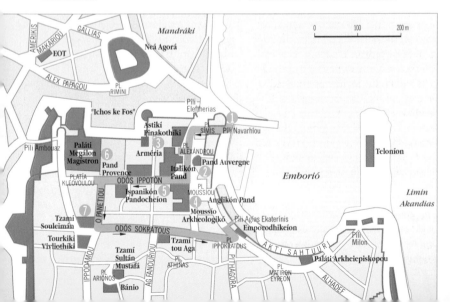

3 Arméria (Arsenal) and Museum of Decorative Arts

The arms of Roger de Pinsot, Grand Master of the Knights of St John from 1355 to 1365, stand above the doorway. The museum contains fine examples of Rhodian pottery, furniture, and traditional costumes.

Leaving Platía Alexándrou by the southwest corner, pause at the Archaeological Museum before turning right on to the long cobbled prospect of Odós Ippóton.

4 Moussío Arkheologikó (Archaeological Museum)

The Archaeological Museum is housed in the former Hospital of the Knights, a grand Gothic building dating from the late 15th century and displaying the arms of Jean de Lastic, Grand Master from 1437 to 1454. The museum, housed on the lower floor, displays a fine assortment of statuary, including the masterly *Aphrodite of Rhodes*, a 1st-century BC statue of the goddess.

5 Odós Ippotón (Street of the Knights)

The eight different 'tongues' all had their lodges (or inns) on this long street, leading uphill from the Hospital and Arsenal to the Palace of the Grand Masters. Turrets, gargoyles, and carved coats of arms above each arched doorway mark the inns of each 'tongue'.

6 Paláti Megálon Magistron (Palace of the Grand Masters)

Square towers, crenellated walls, and sturdy bastions protect the fortress-like palace. The first-floor state rooms contain marvellously restored Hellenic and Roman mosaics.

Walk 250m south on Odós Panetiou. The dome of Tzamí Souleïmán (Mosque of Suleiman) is a landmark at its southern end.

7 Tzamí Souleïmán (Mosque of Suleiman)

The building, converted into a mosque in 1522 following Suleiman's conquest of the city, is elegantly decorated in pale yellow and pink. Originally a Church of the Apostles, it has a fine Italian Renaissance gate.

Turn left on to Odós Sokrátous, the town's main shopping street, lined with jewellers, antique and souvenir shops, designer clothes stalls, and leather boutiques. At the foot of Sokrátous, leave the old town by Píli Agías Ekaterínis.

Rhodes Old Town is a living museum of medieval buildings

Minarets and domes among the palm trees are a reminder of Rhodes' Turkish past. Unlike mosques elsewhere in the islands, some of those on Rhodes are still used by worshippers. Rhodes has quite a large Muslim population, originally dating from the 16th-century conquest, and boosted in 1913 by Greek and Turkish Muslims driven from their homes on Crete in an early act of ethnic cleansing following its union with Greece. They settled in Rhodes, and the Néa Kritika (New Cretan) district on the road to the airport is still a largely Muslim community.

The colourful Tzamí Souleïmán (Mosque of Suleiman) is one of Rhodes' Old Town's major landmarks, while the leaning, turban-topped headstones of the overgrown Muslim cemetery (near the junction of Eleftherias and Vassileos Konstantinou, west of Mandráki harbour) are another relic.

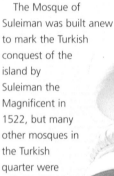

The Mosque of Suleiman was built anew to mark the Turkish conquest of the island by Suleiman the Magnificent in 1522, but many other mosques in the Turkish quarter were

originally Orthodox churches, and fine Byzantine frescoes have been discovered beneath plaster in the disused Pegial el Din and Ilk Mihrab mosques.

On Sokrátous, the shopping street in the heart of the Old Town, the Aga Mosque is still used by local devout Muslims, and other surviving mosques, such as Platía Aronos, in the old quarter, are dotted around the Old Town, which became a purely Muslim quarter after the Turkish conquest.

Greece's Muslim legacy can be seen on Rhodes, Kós, and Crete. Far left: Turkish cemetery, Rhodes Old Town; left: minaret of the Defterdar Mosque, Kós Town; above: the Suleiman Mosque, Rhodes Old Town; right: the Mosque of Nerantzies, Rethimnon, Crete

Walk: Kós Old Town

One of the charms of the island capital is the clutter of medieval and ancient sites painstakingly uncovered after the 1933 earthquake. This easy walk takes in the highlights (*see pp91–3*).

Allow 2 hours.

Start from the south side of the harbour, beneath the castle, whose ramparts are the town's most obvious landmark.

1 Kástro
(Castle of the Knights of St John)

Inner and outer ramparts were built between 1450 and 1478 using many blocks looted from ancient temples. Impregnable towers at each corner strengthen the mighty defences, and with this castle and its twin at Halikarnassos (modern Bodrum, Turkey) the Knights controlled the strategic strait between Kós and the mainland.

Leave the castle by the wooden footbridge, crossing the dry moat to reach Platía Tou

Platanou, the small square leading to the first archaeological site.

2 Platía Tou Platanou
(Hippokrates' Tree)

The giant plane tree, its great boughs spreading to shade the entire square, clings stubbornly to life although its trunk is completely hollow and its branches are supported by scaffolding. To have shaded Hippokrates, it would have to be more than 2,400 years old, making it, perhaps, the oldest tree in Europe.

Cross the square to enter the first of the Old Town's two archaeological sites.

3 Agorá Archaeological Site

This was the site of the Roman town and it was strikingly designed with a flight of broad steps connecting it with the harbour. The street plan, including foundations of temples and civic buildings and paving from ancient streets, can be clearly seen. Nearby, within the same site, are the foundations of the *agorá* (Hellenic marketplace), including the toppled columns and column bases of several temples.

Leave the site by the Platía Eleftherias gate. The Archaeological Museum is on the north side of the square, signposted.

Tumbled columns lie within the medieval Castle of the Knights

4 Moussío Arkheologikó (Archaeological Museum)

A rich and varied collection of Roman and Hellenic sculpture depicts Hippokrates, Hygieia (Goddess of Health), and Hermes (messenger of the gods), while a colourful mosaic of Hippokrates and Asklipios (the god of healing) decorates the courtyard.

5 Defterdar Mosque

The dome and minaret of the Defterdar Mosque, built in the 18th century, stand above Platía Eleftherias on its south side. The arcaded ground floor of the once-grand mosque is occupied by small shops.

Leave Platía Eleftherias by the west side, turning on to the pedestrian Odós Ifestou.

6 Odós Ifestou (Bazaar)

Originally the heart of the medieval Turkish bazaar area, the modern pedestrian street is mainly taken up by souvenir stores and jewellery boutiques. Reminders of the Turkish era include a fountain with Koranic inscription (where Ifestou meets Venizelou), and a lone minaret close to the west end of Ifestou. *At the west end of Ifestou, cross Platía Dhiagoras to enter the town's second archaeological site.*

7 Odeion and Archaeological Site

The lively mosaics and wall paintings uncovered in the ruins of 3rd-century AD Roman houses are the main attraction of this site. Other highlights are the pillars of the ancient gymnasium and the beautifully restored Nymphaion, which dates from the 4th century BC.

With its mosaics, well, and statues, it was first thought by archaeologists to be a sanctuary to all the goddesses. Only later was it discovered to be a lavishly decorated public urinal!

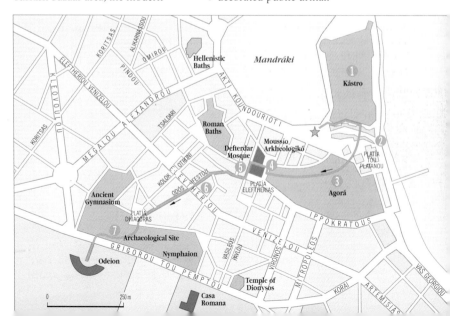

Northeast Aegean Islands

The islands of the northeast Aegean are more remote from Athens and further from each other than those of the cluttered southern waters.

Each has its own strong identity, and the region offers a rich choice of scenic splendours, from the verdant vineyards of Sámos to the rocky magnificence of Mount Fengári on Samothráki, and the treeless hills of Límnos.

Striking village architecture, broad landscapes, and a wealth of medieval sights add to the highly individual charm of each island, while the long coastlines hide many of Greece's least-explored beaches.

Fertile farmlands make the larger northeastern isles prosperous – Sámos is famous for its wine, and Lésvos (Lesbos) and Chíos are renowned for their *ouzo*. Life here has been kinder than on less favoured islands.

The Turkish coast is never far off – it lies within a few kilometres of Lésvos, Sámos, and Chíos – and a strong military presence on several of the islands is a constant reminder of continuing tension between Greece and Turkey.

Since oil was discovered beneath the ocean floor (Greece's only oil rig stands off Thásos), Turkey has renewed claims to mineral rights on the continental shelf. These claims are strenuously denied by Greece.

The northeast Aegean islands joined free Greece only in 1912, after the Greek victory in the First Balkan War.

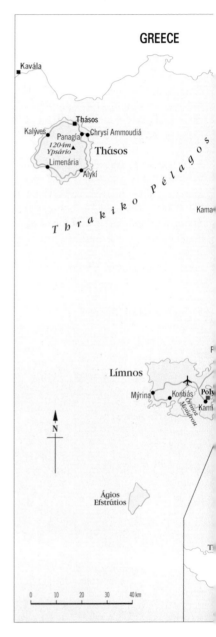

Northeast Aegean Islands

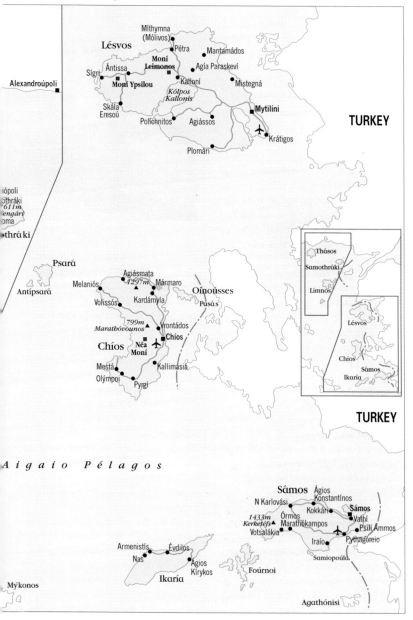

Míthymna (Mólivos)
Lésvos
Pétra
Mantamádos
Moní Leimonos
Agía Paraskeví
Sígri
Ántissa
Kalloní
Mistegná
Alexandroúpoli
Moní Ypsilou
Kólpos Kallonís
Mytilíni
TURKEY
Skála Eresoú
Poliéhnitos
Agiássos
Krátigos
Plomári

iópoli
othráki
1611m
engári
oma

thráki

Psará

Thásos
Samothráki
Límnos

Antípsará
Melaniós
Agiásmata
1297m
Mármaro
Oínoússes
Lésvos
Volissós
Kardámyla
Pásás
Chíos
Sámos
799m
Marathóvounos
Vrontádos
Ikaría
Chíos
Néa Moní
Chíos
Mestá
Kallimasiá
Olýmpoi
Pyrgí
TURKEY

Aigaio Pélagos

Sámos Ágios Konstantínos
N Karlovási
Kokkári
Sámos
1433m
Órmos
Vathí
Kerketéfs
Marathókampos
Psilí Ámmos
Votsalákia
Iraío
Pythagóreio
Armenistís
Évdilos
Samiopoúla
Nas
Ágios Kírykos
Foúrnoi
Ikaría
Mýkonos
Agathónisi

CHIÓS (Khios)

Chíos is a long, crescent-shaped island close to the Turkish coast. Its biggest attractions lie in the high, rolling hinterland of the south, where a handful of unique fortified villages are hidden in fertile pockets among steep hillsides. The island has no outstanding ancient sites, but it possesses a wealth of medieval sites from a richly textured past which blends Byzantine, Genoese, Venetian, and Turkish influences.

A century of Venetian rule (1204–1304) was followed by the long reign of the Genoese Giustiniani family (1346–1566). The massacre of over 25,000 islanders after a failed revolt in 1822 was immortalised by the French painter Eugène Delacroix (1798–1863), and hardened European support for Greece against the Turks.

The majority of the island's most interesting sights and its best beaches are in the southern half of the island, south and west of the capital, Chíos. *75km south of Lésvos.*

Chíos Town (Chóra)

The capital is a busy commercial port and is not much concerned with tourism, though a handful of old streets and buildings lend it character. *Midway along the east coast, facing Turkey.*

Byzantino Moussío (Post-Byzantine Museum/Medjitie Djami)

The courtyard of this former mosque encloses a fascinating array of objects, from green bronze cannon bearing Venetian crests, to Jewish and Turkish tombstones.

The 11th-century Néa Moní stands among cypress trees

Kanari 9, opposite public gardens. Open: Tue–Sun 10am–1pm. Free admission.

Dimotikos Kipos (Public Gardens)

A ring of mature palms surrounds a pair of marble heraldic gryphons and a heroic bronze statue of Konstantinos Kanaris (1822), one of the leaders of the War of Independence. *Town centre. Free admission.*

Kástro (Castle)

The dilapidated walls of the castle quarter (now being restored in places) enclose tumbledown Turkish shop-houses of great charm. The turban-topped tombstones of a Turkish cemetery, shaded by palms, mark the corner of Odós Mit Arseniou and Odós Tzon Kenenty (John Kennedy), while the clustered domes of a derelict medieval *hammam* (Turkish bath) may be seen built into the ramparts at the north end of Navarchos Nikodimou. Ringed by a

now-dry moat, the castle was built in the 10th century AD by the Byzantines and added to by later conquerors.
West end of Neoreion, one block west of the waterfront. Free admission.

Moussío Philippou Argentis (Philip Argentis Museum)

A rich collection of etchings, drawings, traditional costumes, and wooden furniture and utensils.
Korai 2, in the Bibliothiki Khiou Korai (Korai Library). Tel: (0271) 44246. Open: Mon–Thu 8am–2pm, Fri 8am–2pm & 5.30–7.30pm, Sat 8am–12.30pm. Admission charge.

Mastikokhoria (Mastic Villages)

The mastic bush, which grows semi-wild all over southern Chíos, was a source of great wealth in medieval times and is still harvested for its gum, which is used as a base for sweets and perfumes, and is claimed to have medicinal properties. The unique, fortified Mastikokhoria are walled labyrinths, planned for easy defence against raiders.
35–45km southwest of Chíos Town.

Mestá

The best preserved 'mastic village' is a *kasbah*-like maze of warmly coloured stone alleyways and arches surrounding a lovely central square.
10km northwest of Pyrgí.

Néa Moní (New Monastery)

The monastery, built in the 11th century by the Byzantine Emperor Constantine Monomachos, is the finest of its type in Greece. Its striking mosaics are its biggest attraction.

15km west of Chíos Town. Open: daily 6am–1pm & 4–8pm. Free admission.

Olýmpoi

Olýmpoi has grown up around a 13th-century core of walls, with a 20-m defensive tower in its central square. The arched gate of Kato Porta was originally the only way into the village.
5km northwest of Pyrgí.

Pyrgí

Pyrgí's maze of alleys and tall, balconied houses covered with elaborate, dazzling geometric designs, called *xista*, is striking. Clusters of tomatoes and peppers, hung to dry from balconies, add splashes of vermilion.
35km southwest of Chíos Town.

A Pyrgí bakery decorated with geometric patterns

IKARÍA

Long, thin, and very mountainous, Ikaría lies midway between green Sámos and chic Mýkonos (*see p60*), and most island-hoppers bypass it on their way from one to the other. It is said to be where Ikaros (Icarus), son of the legendary Minoan inventor Dedalos (Daedalus), plummeted to his death after flying too close to the sun, thereby melting the wax which held his newly-made wings together. Others who have landed here unwillingly include the composer of the ubiquitous theme tune from *Zorba the Greek*, Mikis Theodorakis, one of many left-wing dissidents confined to Ikaría by pre- and post-war dictatorships.

Ikaría's south coast looks like one long cliff, with its only anchorage at Ágios Kírykos, the island's main port and capital, at its east end. The north coast is almost equally rugged, but the cliffs are broken by deltas of farmland at the mouths of steep valleys. The extensive pine woodlands of Ikaría's inland plateau have been badly damaged by fire, but the island's hinterland is otherwise surprisingly verdant. Like Sámos, it is watered by small, constantly flowing streams.

30km east of Sámos; 50km west of Mýkonos.

Ágios Kírykos

Ikaría's capital, a sleepy village of tumbledown houses, overlooks a fishing harbour and a little-used ferry port.

East end of the south coast.

Armenistís

A fishing hamlet and a row of·tavernas

Quayside at Ágios Kírykos, the main port

overlook a north-facing bay and the best beaches on the island: two long stretches of coarse white sand.

57km west of Ágios Kírykos.

Évdilos

The island's second port is almost derelict, but is coming back to life, thanks to foreign and domestic tourism.

46km northwest of Ágios Kírykos.

Nas

Nas is little more than a name on the map: three tavernas cater for campers and sunbathers on the (unofficial) nude beach in a pebbly, cliff-ringed cove.

4km west of Armenistís.

Naós Artemis Tavropoliou (Sanctuary of Artemis of the Bulls)

Impressive, stepped foundations of this temple overlook a reed-fringed freshwater pool.

Immediately above the beach at Nas.
Free admission.

LÍMNOS (Lemnos)

The rolling hills of Límnos are covered with a golden fuzz of pasture and grain fields. It is one of the richest agricultural islands, dotted with the round stone towers of derelict windmills.

Órmos Moúdrou (Moudros Bay) takes a huge bite out of the south coast. This vast, well-sheltered natural harbour made Límnos a strategic base for the British fleet during the Gallipoli campaign of 1915, for the Turkish coast and the Dardanelles are only 60km to the east. For the same reason, Límnos remains highly militarised, with Greek army and navy installations on most of its hilltops and anchorages.
75km northwest of Lésvos; 270km northeast of Peiraías.

Mýrina

The island's cheerfully old-fashioned but well-kept main town is guarded by a Venetian castle, and has two accessible beaches. The bazaar-like shopping area is lined with charming old-fashioned shop-houses.

Arkheologiko Moussío (Archaeological Museum)

Stone-Age and Bronze-Age finds from sites around the island.
On the Romaikos beach-front, 1km west of the harbour. Open: Tue–Sun 8am–2.30pm. Admission charge.

Frourio Nepheli (Nepheli Castle)

A 13th-century Venetian castle with towers and battlements still intact, dramatically located on a crag.
500m west of harbour.
Open: sunrise–sunset. Free admission.

Polyóchni

Traces of one of the oldest settlements in Greece, dating from the fourth millennium BC, are clearly visible here.
33km east of Mýrina, 3km east of Kaminia village. Signposted.
Open: daylight hours. Free admission.

Though relatively undiscovered, Límnos has some fine beaches around its rocky shores

LÉSVOS (Lesbos)

Lésvos, the third largest of all the Greek islands and one of the most populous – with 105,000 people in its 1,630sq km – has a bit of everything. There are fine beaches on its 370-km long coastline, some of them busy, others quite deserted. There are rolling hills covered with olive groves and pastoral lowlands, arid semi-desert landscapes interspersed by oasis-like valleys, and bald summits emerging from pine-forested foothills. There are quiet fishing harbours, even quieter farming villages in the hills, and one breathtakingly pretty historic town turned resort. It even has its own 'sea', the mirror-calm Kólpos Kallonís, which plunges deeply into the southern coastline. There are some 11 million olive trees, and road verges are often lined with yellow clusters of aniseed, a reminder that Lésvos produces some of Greece's best ouzo.

75km southeast of Límnos; 240km northeast of Athens.

Míthymna (Mólivos)

A delightful, charmingly preserved village of pink and grey stone mansions with bright red, green, yellow, and blue woodwork climbs up to the battlements and circular bastions of the Genoese castle – a dramatic sight when floodlit at night. A pebble-and-sand beach runs along the bay east of the village, and fishing boats bob in the small, taverna-ringed harbour.

62km northwest of Mytilíni.

Eressos Arkheologiko Moussío (Archaeological Museum)

This clearly described collection of finds includes charming pottery heads and figurines, barnacle-encrusted clay jars recovered from the seabed, and fascinating photographs depicting the arrival of the Greek forces in 1912.

In the Dhimotikon (town hall). Signposted. Tel: (0251) 22087. Open: Tue–Sun 8am–2.30pm. Admission charge.

Frourio Molyvou (Mólivos Castle)

From the battlements, there are fine views of the village, the surrounding hills and farmland, and the nearby Turkish coast.

Above the village. Open: Tue–Sun 7.30am–8pm. Free admission.

Moní Ypsilou (Ipsilo Monastery)

A fortified eyrie, dedicated to Áyios Ioannis Theológos (St John the Divine). Arcaded cells surround a cobbled courtyard and church, and its walls are partly decorated with bright blue tiles. A small museum on the second floor displays gorgeous embroidered vestments and illustrated manuscripts.

80km west of Mytilíni on the road to Sígri. Open: daily. Free admission to the museum.

Moní Leimonos (Limonos Monastery)

Constructed in 1527, this is a graceful, rambling building of decorative brick cloisters and grey and pink stone. Its three-room museum displays embroidered robes and crowns, jewellery, icons, and reliquaries.

45km west of Mytilíni, 400m south of main east–west road. Open: 9am–1pm & 5–7.30pm. Admission charge to museum.

Mytilíni

The island capital is a commercial centre with a population of 25,000. Its visitor appeal is threefold – a bustling, eastern-flavoured bazaar area along Odós Ermou, an impressive stronghold, and several excellent museums.

Arkheologiko Moussío (Archaeological Museum)

Statues, pottery, and other finds from local sites.
South end of 8 Novembriou. Tel: (0251) 22087. Open: daily 8am–2.30pm. Admission charge.

Kástro (Castle)

Reconstructed by the Genoese Gattelusi family in 1373, crumbling walls surround the hilltop crowned by massive round towers.
On the eastern promontory, north of the ferry harbour. Open: Mon–Fri 7.30am–3pm. Admission charge.

Moussío Laiki Texnis (Museum of Popular Art)

Village costumes and other memorabilia in a charmingly restored former harbourmaster's office.
Platía Sapphous, on the waterfront. Open: daily (summer only) 10am–1pm. Admission charge.

Moussío Theophilou (Theophilos Museum)

The self-taught Naïve painter Theophilos (1873–1934), who was born on Lésvos, wandered all over Greece painting. This collection includes more than 80 of his landscapes, scenes from mythology, folklore, and village life.

4km from the town centre in Varia suburb. Signposted. Tel: (0251) 28179. Open: Tue–Sun 8.30am–3pm & 4.30–8pm. Admission charge.

Pétra

A long, coarse-sand beach and small resort popular for its proximity to Míthymna.
5km south of Míthymna.

Skála Eresoú (Eressos)

A small resort on the island's best beach, backed by harsh mountains, and an oasis-like delta of fertile farmland.
92km southwest of Mytilíni.

Tall, 19th-century buildings overlook Mytilíni's long sweep of waterfront

Sámos

Sámos is the most popular holiday island in the northeast Aegean and one of Greece's most startlingly beautiful islands. To anyone arriving from the stark, arid landscapes of the Cyclades or the Dodecanese, Sámos is strikingly verdant, with dark green cypress spires rising from slopes covered with poplars, plane trees, and creepers.

Walkers in the narrow streets of Sámos

Set among this natural beauty are prosperous villages which, with their red tiles, white walls, and square stone-built bell towers, could be in Italy.

The island's abundant greenery owes much to its geology: streams and springs emerge from its granite rock to water the vineyards which account for much of the island's income, and Samaina, the dry white wine made by the Coopérative des Vinicoles de Sámos (Sámos Viticulturists' Cooperative), is perhaps the only Greek wine which will bear international comparison.

In antiquity, and especially under the rule of Polykrates (c.536–522 BC), Sámos was a great naval power. It entered the 'tourism' business early, for it was already a popular holiday destination in the Roman era of the 2nd and 1st centuries BC. After rule by the Byzantines, Franks, Venetians, and Genoese, it fell to the Turks in 1475, and despite gaining limited self-rule after 1832 – as an autonomous principality within the Ottoman Empire – it did not join Greece until 1912.

Surprisingly, Sámos has little to show for its glorious and exciting past. Its charm lies instead in its landscapes and in its beaches, which include lovely stretches of dazzling white pebbles on the north coast and some excellent sandy strands on the eastern and southern shores.

210km east of Peiraías.

Sámos

Ágios Konstantínos

A leafy Italianate village spread out along several kilometres of pebble beach on the main north coast road, Ágios Konstantínos is near Kokkári the start for exploring the cypress-covered slopes and network of paths inland (*see pp128–9*).
Midway along the north coast.

Iraío

The white fluted column of the Temple to Hera marks both the island's most important classical site and the tiny, newly-built resort which has sprung up on the pebbly bay next to it.
13km southwest of Pythagóreio.

Naós Iraío (Temple of Hera)

This site is extremely old, with evidence of Mycenaean-era settlement as early as the second millennium BC. The lone column of the great 23-m high temple devoted to Hera, wife of Zeus, is undeniably striking, but the site is confusing and there are no descriptive signs to help you make sense of it.
500m east of the modern village of Iraío. Tel: (0273) 61177. Open: Tue–Sun 8.30am–3pm. Admission charge, unless closed for further excavation.

Karlovási

The island's sprawling western port and commercial centre has few sights of note, though two snarling Venetian marble lions stand in its public gardens, near the town centre. Karlovási's main importance is that it is as an arrival and departure point for island-hopping.
45km west of Vathí, on the north coast.

Kerketéfs Óros (Mount Kerkis)

At 1,433m, this is one of the highest peaks in the Aegean, and its bald dome dominates all of western Sámos. Keen walkers can follow the steep track from the south coast road to the summit.
West end of Sámos; summit track. Signposted to Evangelístria from the coast road west of Votsalákia.

The small castle at Pythagóreio overlooks the sea

Kokkári
A delightfully picturesque fishing village-cum-resort, recognisable from scores of postcards and holiday brochures. There are pebbly beaches and coves to the west of the village.
20km west of Vathí, on the north coast.

Órmos Marathókampos
This pleasant, peaceful village has a thriving boat-building industry which turns out traditionally built wooden *caïques* for local fishermen. It lies at the western end of a long, almost deserted bay with pebbly beaches. To the west looms the often cloud-capped summit of Kerketéfs.
20km south of Karlovási.

Psilí Ámmos
Confusingly, Sámos has two beaches by this name. Both are excellent, sandy bays.
Psilí Ámmos (west) is the less crowded, with almost a kilometre of fine sand, facing south.
5km west of Órmos Marathókampos.
Psilí Ámmos (east) has around 400m of sand, usually invisible beneath dozens of sunbathing bodies.
8km northeast of Pythagóreio.

Pythagóreio
The third of Sámos's three ports is only 10km from the Turkish coast, and is the departure point for day trips to the Turkish resort of Kusadasi. Tavernas cluster the quayside of an enormous harbour where yachts outnumber fishing boats. The remnants of the 6th-century BC city walls can be seen curving around the harbour and the hills behind

the village. These are almost the only indication that this is the site of the great ancient city of Sámos. Pythagóreio has been so-named since 1955, after Pythagoras, the classical-era mathematician who formulated the famous theorem that the square of the hypotenuse of a right-angled triangle is equal to the sum of the squares on the other two sides. Born here in the 6th century BC, and a protégé of the tyrant Polykrates, he later emigrated to the Greek colonies in southern Italy.
Southeast corner of Sámos.

Arkheologiko Moussío (Archaeological Museum)
Finds from the Iraío site (*see p121*), including busts of Roman emperors and a 1st-century BC statue of Augustus Caesar, are the highlights.
In village hall. Tel: (0273) 61400.
Open: Tue–Sun 8am–2.30pm.
Free admission.

Kástro (Castle of Lykurgos Logothetes)
This miniature castle was built in 1824 by the leader of the island's rebellion against the Turks. Around it are the remains of colonnaded houses from the Roman era.
In the centre of the village, 400m west of the harbour. Free admission.

Samiopoúla
The uninhabited islet of Samiopoúla nestles close to its parent island, Sámos. Covered in pines, and with several pretty pebbly coves, it is a pleasant destination for picnics, swimming, and snorkelling trips, which are usually organised by boat operators from

Pythagóreio to its east, and Órmos
Marathókampos to its west.
5km south of Órmos Marathókampos.

Vathí

The island's capital straddles a long inlet
at the eastern end of the north coast.
Built in the 19th century, its Neo-
Classical buildings with their grandiose
façades, the fountain, and palm trees in
the waterfront *platía* have a certain
faded elegance.

Arkheologiko Moussío
(Archaeological Museum)

This houses the largest known free-
standing Greek statue, a 5-m tall figure
of a youth, apparently dedicated to
Apollo, excavated at the Iraío site. The
cauldrons, decorated with bronze
gryphons, on display here are unique to
Sámos.
*In the square at the east end of Kapetan
Katavani. Tel: (0273) 27469.*

*Open: Tue–Sun 8am–2.30pm.
Admission charge.*

Byzantino Moussío
(Byzantine Museum)

An assortment of icons, chalices, holy
vessels, bones of saints, and parchment
manuscripts is on display here.
*In the Mitropoli (Cathedral), one block
back from the waterfront, between
Asklipiadou and 28 Oktobriou.
Open: Tue–Sun 8am–2.30pm.
Admission charge.*

Dimotiki Pinakothiki
(Municipal Art Gallery)

Collection of portraits of grandly
dressed princes of 19th-century Sámos
and bewhiskered heroes of the War of
Independence (1821–30).
*Above the post office in the square at the
east end of Kapetan Katavani, next to the
town hall. Open: daily 8am–2.30pm.
Free admission.*

Sámos has the most wooded landscapes in the Aegean islands

SAMOTHRÁKI

The egg-shaped isle of
Samothráki rises to the
central peak of Mount
Fengári, the highest
mountain in the Aegean
islands at 1,611m. On its
lower northern slopes lies
fertile farmland where
almost all the island's
people work and live. The
grain fields, sheepfolds,
and dense woodland of
this well-watered north
coast are in sharp contrast
to the jagged outlines of
Fengári's peaks and the
near-desert wilderness
of the southeast of the
island.
*45km south of the mainland
port of Alexandroúpoli.*

Kamariótissa

The island's main village is
close to its western tip.
Ferries and hydrofoils link
Samothráki to the main
land, and to the isles to the
north and south.
*Close to the western tip of
the island.*

Palaiópoli

The site of the island's
original capital, abandoned
in the post-Byzantine
period, and now the
location of the most
impressive archaeological
site in the northeast
Aegean.

Ieron ton Megalon Theon (Sanctuary of the Great Gods)

The huge hillside site is
second only to the Minoan
sites on Crete for sheer
impact. High points
include the plinth of the
Rotunda of Arsinoë, and
the five surviving columns
of the Hieron, plus
remnants of the theatre,
the sanctuary's massive
fortifications, and other
shrines.
*6km northeast of
Kamariótissa, signposted to
the Archaeological Museum
from the coast road.
Open: Tue–Sun 8am–
2.30pm. Admission charge.*

Moussío Arkheologiko (Archaeological Museum)

Finds from the site include
altars and friezes, votive
offerings, lovely delicate
Roman glassware, tinsel-
like gold jewellery, 5th-
century BC black-figure
pottery columns from the
Rotunda of Arsinoë, and a
replica of the Winged
Victory of Samothráki (the
original was removed by
French archaeologists in
1863, and is now in the
Louvre, Paris).
*6km northeast of
Kamariótissa. Signposted
from the coast road.
Opening hours and*

THE CULT OF THE GREAT GODS

The colonists from
Sámos who arrived
on Samothráki around
700 BC found that the
island was already settled
by earlier people who had
their own religion.

The Samians absorbed
the local gods into their
own pantheon, creating
in the process the hybrid
cult of the Great Gods,
and they built a vast
sanctuary as their place of
worship.

The cult survived for
almost a millennium,
remaining popular well
into Roman times, partly
because, unlike other
cults of the time, it was
open to women and
slaves, as well as the
ruling class.

Its pantheon was
descended from pre-
Greek Thracian fertility
deities and included the
Great Mother, a
consort named Kadmilos,
and two enigmatic
intercessor gods, the
Kabiroi. These gods were
later identified with the
Dioscouri of the classical
Greek pantheon.

admission charge same as Sanctuary of the Great Gods.

Samothráki Town (Chóra)

Samothráki's tiny medieval capital stands at the head of a hidden valley on the lower slopes of the island's central massif. It is a pretty jumble of two-storey, white, stone houses with painted shutters and red-tiled roofs, crowned by a ruined Byzantine-Genoese castle.
5km from Kamariótissa.

Kástro (Castle)

Round and square bastions surround a tiny square inner keep with a beautiful view down into a wooded valley to the sea and over to the coast of Thrace (Thráki) on the mainland. Marble slabs carved with Byzantine inscriptions and heraldic devices decorate the walls. The

lower storey is the police station.
On the crag above the village.
Free admission.

Laografiko Moussío (Folk Museum)

Traditional implements include a wooden loom and spinning wheel, plus pottery and vividly coloured embroideries.
Above the public library, by the main square, and immediately below the Church of the Virgin. Open: daily 9am–1pm & 7–9pm. Admission charge.

Naós tis Kimisis (Church of the Virgin)

This enormous, whitewashed church, built in 1875, houses the skulls of the Five Martyrs of Samothráki, early Christian saints of the Orthodox faith.
Centre of the village. If closed, inquire at the public library next door for keys.

Marble columns stand above the Sanctuary of the Great Gods

THÁSOS (Thassos)

A circular island of low hills and gentle valleys, Thásos is one of Greece's greener isles – though not as green as it once was. Its pine forests are only now recovering from forest fires which struck in the 1980s, and many of its slopes, especially those on the west side of the island, are cloaked in young, newly-planted trees. A single road makes a 100-km circuit round Thásos, with giddying switchbacks through the hills of the east coast.

Thásos is picturesque and little-visited

Thásos has a couple of quiet resorts, and one outstanding beach, but hasn't yet been discovered by tourism in a big way, despite the fact that international charter flights bring package tourists to mainland Kavála, a mere 30-minute ferry hop away.

25km southeast of mainland port of Kavála.

Alykí

This delightful one-time fishing hamlet is no more than a row of white cottages roofed with slabs of grey stone. It is situated on a tiny isthmus leading to a pine-covered headland, hemmed in by a diminutive sandy beach on its west side, with a clear bay and a pebbly beach on its east flank.

52km south of Thásos Town by road.

Sanctuary of the Dioscuri

Column stumps, walls and foundations, and a stone sarcophagus mark this 7th-century BC site. On the headland immediately above are the ruins of two 5th-century AD Christian churches.

50m west of the village. Signposted. Free admission.

Chrysí Ammoudiá

This gorgeous sweep of coarse white sand and clear water is ringed by dramatic, pine-clad limestone cliffs rising towards the 1,204-m peak of Ypsário, and the 1,100-m summit of Profítis Ilías. The small resort of Chrysí Ammoudiá is at the north end of the beach, with a gaggle of tavernas and houses. Another resort, Skála Potamias, lies at the south end.

7–9km from Thásos Town.

International Symposium for Marble Sculpture

A surprising collection of modern abstract sculpture sitting among the dunes includes a striking white totem pole, a mirror-mosaic cube, and a glass-studded pyramid.

At the north end of Chrysí Ammoudiá beach. Free admission.

Limenária

The island's biggest holiday resort comprises a cluster of shops, tavernas, and small hotels, along a sandy bay on the south coast.

55km south of Thásos Town.

Thásos Town (Limenas)

Thásos Town, the island's capital, is located on a double bay facing the mainland (at its nearest it is only 11km away), with a deep modern ferry harbour and a shallow old harbour. It is a pleasant, sleepy little modern town that is ringed by ancient walls, dotted with spectacular Hellenic remains, and overlooked by a medieval castle. The massive walls of ancient Thásos date from 495 BC and form a 2-km hilltop ring around Limin (don't confuse Limenas with Limenária).
North coast of Thásos.

Agion Apostolon (Holy Apostles)

A small, modern, whitewashed church stands amid the ruins and columns of an early Christian basilica, itself built from remnants of a pre-Christian shrine.
On the headland above the boatyard, 500m east of the old harbour. Free admission.

Agorá (Ancient Marketplace)

The grand ground plan of Hellenic (3rd to 1st century BC) Thásos can clearly be seen, with column bases marking the arcades of the great *stoas* and other buildings.
By the old harbour. Open: Tue–Fri 8am–7pm, weekends 8.30am–3pm. Admission charge.

Arkheologiko Moussío (Archaeological Museum)

This fine collection includes the *Kriophoros of Thásos*, a giant archaic statue, dating from the 6th century BC, of a naked youth carrying a ram to sacrifice. There are also terracotta works, and marble and ivory carvings.
Next to the agorá. *Open: Tue–Fri 8am–7pm, weekends 8.30am–3pm. Admission charge.*

Arkheo Theatro (Ancient Theatre)

This marble-tiered theatre is still used in summer, when music and drama performances take advantage of the perfect acoustics.
750m above the agorá. *Free admission.*

Kástro (Castle)

The battlements of a medieval Genoese castle surmount the city walls at their highest point.
1km west of Agion Apostolon, 250m from Arkheo Theatro. Free admission.

The ancient theatre at Thásos Town, used for performances in the summer

Walk: Hills of Sámos

The hills rising from the north coast of the island combine verdant woodlands with dramatic mountain views and quaint villages. This walk starts and finishes on the coast. If you start by 9am you should arrive back in Kokkári in time for lunch and a lazy afternoon on the beach. The route may be slightly altered by newly-built dirt roads; the walking path is marked with red dots painted on walls and boulders, but you must keep a sharp eye open for these as they can easily be overlooked.

Allow 3–4 hours.

Start at the southwest end of Kokkári, at the junction of the old road through the village and the new bypass, next to the Míos Beach Hotel. Follow the tarred side road which quickly turns into a dirt track, and keep left of the farm fields inland of Kokkári until after 10 minutes the track – now a footpath – passes under a derelict Turkish aqueduct. Continue to follow this trail, crossing two new forestry jeep tracks.

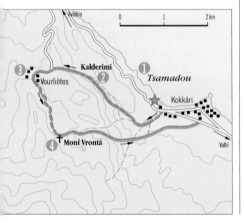

1 Tsamadou

The trail follows the 200-m contour, with the vivid turquoise bay of Tsamadou and its white pebble beach immediately below, to your right. *Continue across a rocky ravine to the base of the final pitch to Vourliótes village.*

2 Kalderimi

The last and steepest stage of the walk follows one of Sámos's surviving *kalderimia*, the painstakingly cobbled mule-paths which once criss-crossed every island but have since been destroyed in many places by new road-building or have simply been neglected. *After 90 minutes, the trail meets the tarred road to Vourliótes. Continue for a further 15 minutes to the village.*

3 Vourliótes

The outskirts of Vourliótes are reminiscent of a ghost town, with the tumbledown walls of abandoned houses lining narrow lanes. In the last century, the village had 1,200 inhabitants. It now has fewer than half that number, but streams and fertile land make the remaining inhabitants prosperous by hill-village standards. Stop for a drink and snack in the quaint central square. *Return to Kokkári via the Moní Vrontá trail, rising to 500m above sea level. Head south on the track (signposted and marked with red dots) which leads from the eastern corner of Vourliótes.*

4 Moní Vrontá (Our Lady of the Thunder)

The substantial, stone-roofed monastery of Vrontá dates from the 16th century, when Sámos – which had been deserted for a century because of pirate raids – was resettled by Greeks from Asia Minor under a benevolent pasha. According to island belief, thunderstorms always follow the festival of the Birth of the Virgin, which is celebrated here and in Vourliótes on 7–8 September each year. (Note: the Greek army sometimes billets troops in the monastery and photography may be banned if they are in residence.)

From Vrontá, follow the path downhill and northeast from the monastery, signposted Monopati Kokkári (Kokkárivia Footpath). The trail follows the right bank of a deep gorge, with sheer cliffs on the opposite side, and views down to Kokkári. On a clear day, you can see right across to Turkey.

After another 45 minutes, the trail cuts across a web of fields and dirt tracks, passes through olive groves, and emerges at a taverna on the main road, 500m from Kokkári village centre.

Kokkári, where the walk ends, is a quaint combination of resort and fishing village

Old, gnarled, cross-legged fishermen mending bright yellow or dark crimson nets are one of the everyday sights of the Greek islands, and no island harbour is complete without its flotilla of tiny, brightly painted fishing boats.

Almost all of them bear the names of a local saint, who protects both boat and boatmen. This is a very traditional form of life insurance, and is reflected onshore in the tiny chapels dedicated to the Panagía (Virgin), built by grateful fishermen in thanks for their safekeeping and livelihood at sea.

You can see traditional wooden *caïques* being built and repaired in the harbours of Kokkári and Karlovási on Sámos (*see pp121–2*), Sými (*p154*), Thásos Town (Limenas) on Thásos (*p127*), and at other island ports.

If you look closely at the prow of one of these little vessels, you will often see a diamond shape cut into the wood – a stylised version of the eye painted on the prow of the ancient *triremes* and a reminder that the captains of these little fishing-boats are descendants of the

sailors who trounced the Persian fleet at Salamis.

Much fishing is done at night. Flotillas of dinghies, each carrying a pair of powerful gas lamps, are used to attract squid and small fry into circles of nets. The sound of their engines 'putt-putting' back into harbour at first light starts many an island day.

Another oft-heard harbour sound is the slap of an octopus being tenderised by pounding its rubbery tentacles against a boulder. Octopus are taken with a trident or a formidable triple hook on a handline.

On most islands, the catch is as small as the boats. Overfishing has taken its toll of Aegean stocks. Island boatmen pursue their quarry with everything from fine-mesh nets to spear-guns and fish-traps. Dynamite was sometimes used to maximise impact, and it is not uncommon to meet an older fisherman who has lost a hand through mis-handling of explosives. These days, more environmentally friendly fish farms are widely established in an effort to increase island fish stocks.

Tourism, and ever-increasing prosperity in Greece itself, have played a part in encouraging intensive fishing. Greeks and tourists love fresh fish, and prices for the prized *barbounia* (red mullet) have soared.

Finally, on island beaches you may see fishermen of another sort: young

Romeos who spend their summers in pursuit of female tourists are called *kamaki* – 'harpooners'.

Some things hardly change, though engines and nylon nets make life easier

Sporádes and Évvoia (Evia)

The gentle, pine-cloaked Sporádes, with their mild summers, superb beaches, and postcard-pretty villages, are easy to fall in love with at first sight. An archipelago of rocky, uninhabited islets lies around the four main isles, each of which has a distinct character of its own.

Skýros Town stands below a rocky crag crowned by a fortified monastery

Three of the four Sporádes islands – Skíathos, Skópelos, and Alónnisos – are within sight of each other and connected by a fast hydrofoil service

The fertile farmlands of Évvoia are a chequerboard of grain fields and olive groves

which also links them with the port of Vólos within the Pagasitikós Kólpos (Pagasitic Gulf) on the mainland. The fourth, Skýros, is far to the southeast, off the eastern shore of the wooded, fertile island of Évvoia, which lies within a few kilometres of the mainland coast. The four Sporádes have just enough visitable history to make them interesting, being scattered as they are with deserted villages, medieval monasteries, and Venetian fortifications.

Their real appeal, however, lies more in their idyllic beaches, gentle landscapes, and relative lack of mass-market tourism.

Skíathos, with an international airport, is the busiest, but out of the peak holiday season, its dozens of sandy beaches offer enough space for everyone. Skópelos has only recently been discovered by the holiday industry, while Alónnisos, Skýros, and Évvoia remain well off the beaten track.

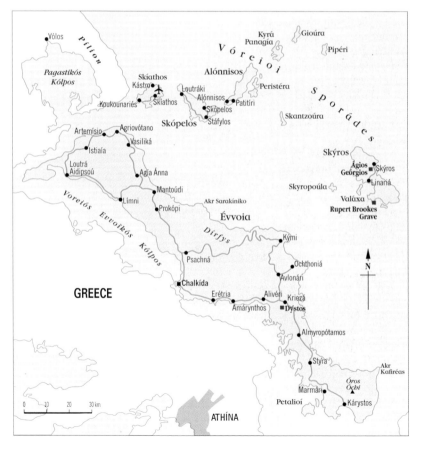

ALÓNNISOS

Alónnisos is the quietest and remotest of the three western Sporádes. Hillier and less greenly forested than its neighbours, it is also the most sparsely inhabited isle. In 1965, an earthquake rocked its main village, and the islanders relocated to Patitíri, now the island's harbour and main centre. Much of the coast is lined with steep, eye-catching cliffs, and its scattering of beaches – some sandy, some pebbly, none crowded – are best approached by boat. In summer, small craft ply from Patitíri, saving a long, hot trek.

A Byzantine shipwreck has been found on the sea bed near the island, and the rare Mediterranean monk seal lives around the uninhabited islets north of Alónnisos. As a result, the waters north of the island have been declared a marine conservation area, and we would urge you to boycott trips to sea caves which may be used by the seals (*see p156*).
25km east of Skíathos.

Alónnisos Town (Chóra)

Abandoned after the earthquake, when the government relocated its inhabitants to Patitíri, this delightfully pretty village is coming back to life, mainly as a result of its charming but derelict houses being bought by Athenians and foreigners who restore them as holiday homes. Islanders are outnumbered by English and German residents, and Alónnisos Town really only comes to life in July and August. *Inland of the west coast, close to the southern point of the island.*

Kalamakia

A long stretch of pebbly, sandy beach with several small seasonal tavernas. *East coast, 8km north of Patitíri.*

Kokkinokástro

A lovely pebble beach, surrounded by hills, cliffs, and pinewoods, Kokkinokástro has been identified as the site of the oldest prehistoric settlement in the Aegean islands, and excavations have located the remains of ancient Ikos. The site is of more interest to archaeologists than to casual sightseers. Diligent searching reveals the stumps of a short stretch of the city wall near the beach.

THE CYCLOPS

The deserted island of Gioúra, 25km north of Alónnisos, was said to be the home of the Cyclops, the cannibalistic one-eyed giants of Greek mythology. In Homer's epic, the *Odyssey*, one of them, Polyphemus, captured the wandering Odysseus and his crew on their long journey home from the siege of Troy. After Polyphemus had seized and eaten several of his men, Odysseus blinded the monster with a sharpened stake, then craftily escaped from the cave, tied beneath the bellies of the Cyclops' sheep. In his rage, Polyphemus hurled huge boulders at Odysseus' departing ship, thus forming the craggy reefs and islets around Gioúra.

East coast, 5km north of Patitíri
(unmarked), and freely accessible.

Patitíri

Patitíri is a modern settlement, thrown up in a hurry to rehouse villagers from Chóra after the 1965 earthquake. Since then, the Greek islanders' passion for flowers, pot plants, and idiosyncratic decorations of all sorts has done much to personalise the once charmless settlement. Its location, on a calm bay hemmed in by low sandstone bluffs and pine-wooded hillsides, is hard to beat.

A gradually decaying *kalderimi* (cobbled donkey path) leads up a pretty 45-minute hike to Alónnisos town,

situated on the hills above.
East coast, close to the southern end of
the island.

Peristéra

Separated by a narrow strait from Alónnisos, the tiny isle of Peristéra is at times busier than its big sister. In high season, its beaches are a popular destination for day-trips from Skópelos, and even from Skíathos. At other times, its hamlets – Peristéra in the south, and Livádia, an anchorage on the west coast – are usually deserted, and then the island is only for the most demanding of solitude-seekers.

10km northeast of Patitíri.

Many of the pretty houses in old Alónnisos Town have been renovated as holiday homes

ÉVVOIA (Euboea, Evia)

Some say Greece's second largest island (after Crete) hardly qualifies as an island at all. The Gulf of Évvoia (Evvoïkos Kólpos), which separates it from the mainland, narrows to a channel just 100m wide, and you can cross to the mainland by a swing bridge. It is, therefore, not surprising that in some ways Évvoia's atmosphere is more akin to that of the mainland than to its nearest island neighbours.

The Venetian-Greek church of Agía Paraskevi stands in the middle of Chalkída

Holidaymakers looking for the quick island fix offered by the smaller isles will not find Évvoia instantly charming, but explorers who take time to discover it will not go away disappointed.

Inland, Évvoia is a fertile island of wide valleys and thickly wooded hills cloaked in plane and chestnut trees. Beaches on its southwest coast, closest to Athens, are popular resorts for Greek holidaymakers from the mainland. In the north, the Greek fondness for thermal springs has encouraged the growth of several small beach-and-spa resorts. By contrast, the island's steep east coast is dotted with undiscovered beaches and coves, many of them accessible only by boat or by four-wheel-drive vehicle and strictly for self-sufficient beachcombers, as they are without facilities of any kind.

Chalkída (Khalkis)

Chalkída, the island's capital, was important in antiquity, when it controlled the main coastal shipping route from northern to southern Greece, and the whole island was one of the richest Venetian possessions in Greece until its fall to the Turks in 1470.

Today, few visitors linger in this modern, grimy, industrial town for more time than it takes to check out its single natural wonder and visit its medieval stronghold.
West coast of Évvoia, 88km from Athens.

Evrípou

A swing bridge from this point in Chalkída carries the road across the gulf which separates Évvoia from the mainland. Through this narrow channel swirls a current which changes direction several times a day, for reasons which baffled Aristotle (who is said to have plunged into it in frustration) and continue to puzzle scientists even today.
Town centre.

Frourio Karababas (Karababa Fortress)

A grim 17th-century fortress built by the Turks to control the narrows.
Hilltop on the island side of the Evripos bridge, north of road. Free admission.

Dýstos

Above the 5th-century BC ruins, a small Venetian castle crowns a low hill where the acropolis of the ancient city stood.

By the shores of a marshy lake 5km south of Krieza. Signposted. Reached by dirt road from main Chalkída–Kárystos road. Free admission.

Erétria
In ancient times, an important ally of Athens against the Persians, Erétria is now largely concealed beneath the modern village.
21km southeast of Chalkída.

Arkheologiko Moussío (Archaeological Museum)
Pottery finds and bronzes from the site of ancient Erétria.
See Theatrou for location and timings.

Theatrou (Ancient Theatre)
Steps from the theatre descend to a vault. Beside it are the foundations of a sanctuary and gymnasium.

Northwest part of village. Signposted. Tel: (0221) 62206. Open: Tue–Sun 8am–2.30pm. Combined admission charge to museum and site.

Kárystos
This is the main port of southern Évvoia and is a popular summer resort used by mainland Greeks. It has a long sand-and-shingle beach west of the town, and is overlooked by the fine mountain scenery of Mount Ochi (Óros Óchi).
90km southeast of Chalkída.

Kástro (Castle Rosso)
The towering, wind-worn, dark red battlements of the great, empty castle, built by the Venetians in the 13th century, are an impressive sight on the low hill behind the town.
1.5km from Kárystos harbour.
Free admission.

The stone battlements of Castle Rosso loom over Kárystos harbour

SKÍATHOS

Skíathos claims to possess more and better beaches than any other Greek island. The claim is hard to argue with: not only are there enough beaches to give each of its many high-season visitors a fair share of space, but the beaches are made of the finest yellow sand in the Aegean.

Lined with nodding calamus reeds ('Greek bamboo'), and surrounded by pines which scent the island air, these are strands to delight the most demanding beach enthusiast.

The island's popularity is enhanced by an international airport which brings package holidaymakers from northern Europe, and Skíathos is also a popular resort for well-off Athenian villa- and yacht-owners.

All but a few hundred of the island's 4,000 inhabitants live in the only village, called either Skíathos Town or Chóra, but most visitors stay in one of the half-dozen resorts scattered around its 44km of coast.

Unimportant in ancient times, Skíathos passed from the Byzantines to the Venetians in the 13th century, then to the Turks in 1538, before rejoining Greece in 1828. Sightseeing includes pretty hillside monasteries on Skíathos itself, and there are boat and hydrofoil trips to the beautiful Pílion peninsula or the port of Vólos on the mainland, and to the neighbouring islands of the Sporádes group.
64km southeast of mainland port of Vólos.

Kástro

The towering walls and drawbridge of the island's one-time main village defied seaborne raiders from the beginning of the 16th century until 1830, when, with the end of the War of Independence, the islanders felt secure enough to move from their safe but inconvenient clifftop homes to build a new capital at Chóra. The medieval village had 22 churches and about 300 homes. Today, just two of its churches survive.
8km northwest of Skíathos Town. Access on foot or by boat.

Pantokrátor (Church of Christ)

This 17th-century church contains some lovely Byzantine icons and frescoes and a carved iconostasis (icon screen).
Within the walls of the Kástro.
Open: irregular hours.

Koukounariés

This is the longest beach on Skíathos and its top holiday destination, with several large and small hotels. The town offers 1,000m of pine-shaded sand, watersports, and all the accoutrements of a successful resort.
12km southwest of Skíathos Town.

Lalaria

A curved beach of white pebbles is hemmed in by white cliffs half way along the island's north coast. Undeveloped as yet, Lalaria receives a daily seaborne invasion of day-trippers from Koukounariés and Chóra.
8km north of Skíathos Town. Access by boat or dirt road.

Panagía Evangelistrías

Built in the late 18th century, this monastery is best known for its striking

frescoes, which date from 1822.
4km north of Skíathos Town. Open: daily 8am–noon & 5–8pm. Free admission.

Panagía Kounístras

This modest little monastery, founded in 1540 and restored in 1738, has glowing Byzantine icons and frescoes.
6km west of Skíathos Town. Open: daily 8am–1pm & 5–8pm. Admission charge.

Skíathos Town (Chóra)

Built in 1830, with pretty red-tiled houses and a church bell tower, the village looks almost more Italian than Greek. It stands on a pretty double bay which forms two harbours, one for yachts and one for fishing boats. The bay is lined with cafés and restaurants, while offshore the waters are dotted with pine-covered rocks and islets.

Bourtzi

In the middle of the bay, a small Venetian-built castle guards the harbour. *Closed.*

Moussío Papadiamantis (Papadiamantis Museum)

Here in his former home, a small collection of memorabilia commemorates the island's most famous son, novelist, and poet Alexandros Papadiamantis (1851–1911).
Town centre. Signposted. Open: weekdays 8.30am–2pm & 5–8pm.

Koukounariés beach on Skíathos

SKÓPELOS

A long, thin island with a spine of hills covered in fragrant pine woods, Skópelos is dotted with dozens of tiny chapels tucked away in the woods or perched on steep hillsides: there are over 360 little churches in its main village alone. There are up to a dozen convents and monasteries – most of them deserted – scattered around the island.

Steep cliffs give Skópelos striking coastal scenery, but make it less appealing to beach lovers, who flock to nearby Skíathos. Skópelos has an array of delicious white-pebble coves, most of them difficult to access by land, and more easily reached by boat.

Tourism is growing fast, mainly as a result of overspill from nearby Skíathos, whose international airport also brings Skópelos within easy reach. But the island retains its own charm, with small farms growing fruit, olives, and nut trees among the ubiquitous pine forest.
6km east of Skíathos.

Limnonari

An excellent beach of coarse white sand surrounded by pines. The chirping of cicadas in summer is deafening.
9km southwest of Skópelos Town.

Loutráki

Ferries from neighbouring islands call at this northern port as well as at Chóra. Apart from its narrow and mediocre beach, Loutráki has little to offer.
28km northwest of Skópelos Town.

Milia

By far the biggest and best beach on the island, Milia is a 1.5km curve of small

Skópelos Town's churches offer fine views across the bay

white pebbles backed by steep, pine-clad slopes. So far, it remains pleasantly unspoilt.
14km west of Skópelos Town, on the west coast.

Skópelos Town (Chóra)

The town's typical tall houses rise in tiers above a deep, narrow bay surrounded by pine-wooded mountains. With steeply pitched stone roofs and jutting balconies of carved wood and wrought iron, these dignified dwellings are quite different from the cosy red-tiled villas of neighbouring Skíathos or the white cubes of Skýros. Skópelos is full of character. Pleasant tavernas and cafés under green, shady trees line the seaside promenade where generations of islanders stroll at sundown.

Kástro (Castle)

A coat of whitewash makes the tiny, ruined Venetian castle less militaristic than most such island strongholds. There is not much to see inside, but the view over the bay, to the three hillside monasteries opposite, makes the steep walk worthwhile, especially at sunset.

Moní Evangelistrías (Convent of the Evangelist)

This four-columned church, built in 1712, is famed for its superb Byzantine icon of the Panagía (Virgin).
Open: 8am–1pm & 4–7pm.
Free admission.

Moní Metamórphosis (Monastery of the Transformation)

Illuminated manuscripts dating from the post-Byzantine era are the proudest possession of this 16th-century monastery, recently restored to its original splendour.
Open: 8am–1pm & 5–8pm.
Free admission.

Moní Prodrómou (Convent of John the Baptist)

Built in 1721, this monastery features a carved iconostasis and icons, and is located with striking views of the town.
Open: 8am–1pm & 5–8pm.
Free admission.

Stáfylos

The island's prettiest beach is at the foot of a natural amphitheatre of cliffs and steep pine slopes which are dotted with summer tavernas and small hotels. As it is close to Chóra, it is also the most crowded beach, and is lined with colourful umbrellas and loungers in July and August.
6km south of Skópelos Town.

Velanio

To get away from the Stáfylos crowds, take a 10-minute walk east along the shore to the neighbouring beach of Velanio, almost equally attractive but not yet a full-scale resort strip.
6.5km south of Skópelos Town.

The church in Skópelos Town rises like an amphitheatre above the harbour

SKÝROS

Lonely Skýros is the joker in the Sporadic pack. Off to the south and east of its companions, it is an hourglass-shaped island of two faces. North of its narrow waist, its pretty main village looks over empty seaward horizons, pine woods and farmlands fringed with long shingle beaches. The southern half of the island is strikingly different, a jagged lunar landscape of shattered boulders where even the goats have a tough time finding greenery.

Skýros is one of the few islands where some older people still wear distinctive traditional costume, including neatly pleated indigo coloured trousers (*see pp144–5*), and it maintains a strong handicrafts heritage which includes beaten-copper dishes and bowls, decorated ceramics, embroidery, and elaborately carved wooden furniture.

Village homes open straight on to the street, and a walk through the breathtakingly steep lanes of the island's main village allows glimpses into house-proud parlours, decorated and furnished with local products.

Unique to Skýros is a vanishing breed of miniature pony, native since at least the 8th century BC. Once used in the fields, the ponies have been left to fend for themselves with the advent of farm machinery, and their numbers have plummeted to around 200.

24km northeast of Kými on Évvoia.

Linariá

The island port offers some accommodation and has a small beach just north of the harbour.

10km south of Skýros Town.

A jumble of flat-roofed houses of Skýros Town.

Skýros Town (Chóra)

The island's main village is by far the prettiest of the Sporádes' capitals. A jumble of flat-roofed houses beneath a dark crag crowned by a fortified monastery, and the ruins of a 1,000-year-old Byzantine fastness make up this idyllic old-fashioned community. Most summer visitors are Greek, so flashy cocktail bars have not yet supplanted traditional tavernas and cafés, and off the narrow, car-free main street, the town's vertical maze of lanes and alleys is a puzzle. Visitors wander upwards, downwards, and sideways before emerging triumphant at the castle gates. *On the east coast, close to the 'waist' of the island.*

Ágios Geórgios

Founded in the 10th century, and rebuilt in 1680, this monastery has remarkable frescoes of Christ Pantokrator. *Immediately below the castle, entered by an arched gateway below the ramparts. Open: daily 8am–1pm & 5–8pm. Free admission.*

Agía Triáda

The fading glow of this tiny chapel's frescoes should not be missed.
50m below the castle. Open: daily. Free admission.

Brooke Memorial

A bronze statue of a youth symbolising immortal poetry commemorates the English war poet Rupert Brooke (1887–1915), buried on Skýros after his death (of typhus) aboard a naval hospital ship at Moudros. The male nude shocked villagers, who, when it was first unveiled, draped it in sheets.
Signposted from the main street.

Kástro

The age-old Byzantine castle offers fine sunset views over the western hills.
At the highest point of the village, entry via the Ágios Geórgios monastery gateway. Open: daylight hours. Free admission.

Magasia

This long, east-facing beach of coarse sand, within sight of Skýros Town, is reckoned to be the best on the island.
1km northeast of Skýros Town.

Moussío Faltaits

A small folklore museum with an excellent collection of traditional weaving, carving, pottery, and metalwork.
Opposite the statue of Rupert Brooke. Signposted from the village centre. Tel: (0222) 91950/91232. Open: daily 10am–1pm & 5.30–8pm. Admission charge.

Treis Boukes (Rupert Brooke's Grave)

The English war poet is buried in an isolated olive grove on the rocky slopes of southern Skýros.
Overlooking Treis Boukes Bay, 23km southeast of Linariá. Access by boat from Linariá.

Local ceramics and embroideries decorate the parlour of a typical home

In tiny folk museums around the islands you can see the elaborate, colourful costumes of yesteryear: full skirts, embroidered blouses, and slippers for women; loose trousers, knee-boots, and full-sleeved shirts with gold-braided velvet waistcoats for men. Each island has its own special costume, and on more populous islands, such as Lésvos, each village had (or still has) its distinctive dress.

The most lavish outfits are for special occasions – wedding feasts or religious festivals – but there are distinctive workaday clothes too, like the huge, baggy, white cotton shirts and trousers, linen waistcoats, and enormous straw *sombreros* worn by farmers in the Cyclades as recently as 100 years ago.

Sadly, these costumes have all but died out and only vestiges remain. In the wild west of Lésvos, donkey-riding hill farmers still wrap yellow bandanas around their heads, pirate-style, and village women on Chíos favour old-fashioned, snood-like headscarves.

Today, there are just three islands where traditional costume is still worn daily, usually by older men and women. The magnificent, all-black costume of Cretan mountain men is famous, and their knee-length boots, voluminous black pants, shirts, and silk headscarves are still to be admired in the remoter villages of southwest Crete. On Skýros, a few 'good old boys' wear fantastically pleated indigo-dyed trousers, soft pillbox caps, loose collarless shirts, and tube-like sandals.

In the village of Ólympos on Kárpathos (*see pp88–9*), it's the women who keep up traditional appearances, wearing an everyday costume of a long skirt with embroidered bodice and headscarf, while a fancier version comes out for special occasions.

Elsewhere, traditional wear has died out. Men and women alike adopted western European dress long ago, and the only traditional peasant clothing you will see will be from Nepal, Bali, or Guatemala – on the trendy backs of visiting backpackers.

Facing page: young girls in traditional costume on the island of Mýkonos; above: Greek women in their national dress on Ascension Day; right: in full regalia at St Spiridion Procession, Corfu

Getting Away From It All

Greece's most popular islands are of course those that are easiest to reach by air or by direct sea routes which don't involve hours afloat. But there are hundreds more islands, some inhabited by only a few fisher families, others completely deserted, waiting to be discovered. Some may have to wait for a while: infrequent (or non-existent) ferries are a powerful tourism deterrent.

Sea legs are essential for a vacation here

There is no better way to visit these out-of-the-way isles than aboard your own vessel. Take a chartered yacht with an expert crew, and sail in the pampered style of a luxury cruise ship, or jump aboard an old-fashioned island trader converted for island-hopping in comfort.

Caïque Cruises

The smaller islands and inaccessible beaches of the Dodecanese group (*see pp84–5 & pp150–55*) can be visited on one of the graceful wooden vessels called *caïques* which, until the coming of steam, monopolised inter-island trade. Several of these traditional 25-m long motor-sailers have been converted to carry up to 16 passengers, in twin-berth cabins with en-suite hot-water shower and WC. They usually have a crew of four – captain, engineer, steward-deckhand, and cook – and as the price of a one-week cruise includes most meals and drinks, they are very good value for money, costing little more than a one-week package holiday.

Most cruises operate out of Kós or Rhodes, and visit islands between the two. Some cruises also operate north of Kós to Pátmos, and the archipelago of sleepy little islands nearby.

Most companies operate cruises from mid-May to early October only. A list of tour operators offering *caïque* cruises is available from the Greek National Tourist Office (*see pp188–9*).

Island Cruises

Numerous luxury cruise lines operate itineraries from Píreas (the port of Athens). The most popular destinations are much-photographed Mýkonos (*see pp60–61*), Pátmos (*see pp98–9*), Rhodes (*see pp102–7*), and Thíra (Santoríni) (*see pp68–9 & pp72–3*). Itineraries may also include ports of call on the Greek mainland, and in Turkey.

Cruises can be as short as one day (two–three weeks is more common), and may be arranged through local travel agencies or major hotels. Contact: **Dolphin Hellas Cruises**, Akti Miaouli 71, 185 37 Peiraías. *Tel: (01) 512 109.* **Epirotiki Lines**, Akti Miaouli 87, 185 38 Peiraías. *Tel: (01) 4291 000.* **Sun Line**, Iassonos 3, 185 37 Peiraías. *Tel: (01) 4523 417.*

Flotilla Sailing

For less confident sailors, yacht flotillas, with a lead yacht skippered and crewed by professionals, are the ideal way to explore Greek waters for the first time. Flotillas of up to a dozen fully equipped modern yachts sail from several islands. The Ionian islands (*see pp24–45*), with their sheltered waters, many anchorages, and steady breezes, are the most popular for flotilla sailing.

A list of flotilla sailing specialists is available from the Greek National Tourist Office (*see pp188–9*).

Yacht Charter

Steady winds, sunny weather, and literally thousands of island anchorages make Greece a delight for yacht sailors.

There are dozens of yacht charter companies in Greece, based not only in Píreas on the mainland but at marinas throughout the islands. Rhodes is among the most popular bases for charter companies. The government has grandiose plans for a network of new marinas at various mainland and island ports.

The weather is suitable for sailing from April to October, though strong winds can occasionally keep boats in harbour for days at a time in the Cyclades (the most popular yachting area) in August. Crewed and bareboat charters are available.

A full list of yacht charter companies is available from the Greek National Tourist Office (*see pp188–9*).

Allónnios: craft of all sorts ply the blue seas of the Greek islands

Island Flowers

Rocky island slopes look barren in high summer, but in spring and early summer they can be a kaleidoscope of red, yellow, and purple wild flowers. A hillside which in August is a near-monochrome canvas of grey and tan will be vividly splashed with colour in March or April.

The best time to see the islands in bloom is in the spring, which comes as early as March in southern Crete or as late as May to early June in the northeast Aegean isles. On most islands, much land is useful only for goat pasture, and wild flowers are left to flourish without interference – except from the goats. Island farming is piecemeal, with tiny terraced fields growing varied crops instead of the prairie-style monoculture of northern Europe. More than 6,000 species of flowering plants and ferns grow in Greece, far more than in any other European country, and 750 of them are unique to Greece.

Small fields and meadows lie fallow for much of the year, and wild flowers thrive alongside cultivated plants in

fields and olive groves. Poppies, vetches, and a dozen kinds of wild daisy are among the most abundant blooms, with anemones, cyclamen, asphodel, and crocuses blooming in spring and autumn on slopes and in fields.

Throughout the dry summers, stream beds are marked by serpentine lines of pink-flowered oleander bushes, whose poisonous leaves deter even the ever-hungry goats.

The greenish-yellow flowers of fennel (anise) are also summer survivors, seen everywhere in fields and roadsides and harvested to give *ouzo*, the Greek national drink, its distinctive aniseed flavour. Giant fennel, found on stony pastureland, can reach 4m in height.

Island villages are always a blaze of flowers. Not all homes have the luxury of a garden, but all are adorned with fountains of red pelargoniums and bright green basil growing in recycled

olive oil cans. Vines, purple morning glories, and scarlet bougainvillea (imports from South America) make shady arbours, and the violet-flowered derris creeper from Australia is another colourful import.

Facing page: prickly pears grow beside pelargoniums on a village terrace. This page: wild flowers make a dazzling display of colour in the short island spring.

THE SMALLER ISLANDS

Scattered among the bigger, better-known islands are many tinier isles, some with thriving villages, some deserted but for a handful of fishermen. These dots on the map are not always remote in terms of distance. Many are within an hour's sailing of popular resorts and international airports. But reaching them can be a challenge, and it is surprising how crowded some of them can be in high season. Most have one village and a single small beach, and space can be limited in July and August.

Outside the peak months, though, the small isles are a delight for real island fans. If you can be content with a beach, a book, and a simple dinner in an unsophisticated taverna, they offer a sense of peace and isolation – the Greeks call it *isikhia* – that the developed resorts cannot match. And their people, for whom visitors are still something of a novelty, are among the friendliest in Greece.

Agathónisi, Arkoí, and Leipsoí

These three islands, with scores of uninhabited rocks and skerries, form a lovely mini-archipelago in the northern Dodecanese, sheltered from northerly winds by Sámos and an arm of the Turkish coast.

Agathónisi

A long, low, barren isle of fishermen and goatherds, its name means 'thorny island'. Around 150 people live here, and the main village, sheltered among low hills, is simply called Megalo Khorió – 'the big village' – to distinguish it from the even tinier Mikro Khorió.

30km east of Pátmos. Weekly ferries from Pátmos and Sámos (Pythagóreio).

Arkoí

Arkoí, with a population of fewer than 70, lies in the midst of a jumble of even tinier rocks, and on a clear day, with the hills of Pátmos, Ikaría, Sámos, Turkey, and the smaller islands nearby ringing the horizon, it seems to be afloat on an inland lake instead of in the open sea. Its attractions are: superbly clear water, excellent snorkelling, and lots of islets on which to sunbathe and picnic.

10km east of Pátmos. Weekly ferries from Pátmos and Sámos (Pythagóreio).

Leipsoí

Almost 600 people live on Leipsoí, making it the metropolis of this mini-island group. Half a dozen tiny white churches, each with its distinctive blue dome, stand out against the hillside terraces which make the most of each patch of fertile land. The broad harbour is home to a small fishing fleet, and with its shallow, glass-clear water it is a natural aquarium full of colourful fish and other Aegean sea life. A sandy beach, five minutes' walk north of the harbour, is complemented by brilliant white sand coves along the north shore.

8km east of Pátmos; weekly ferries and frequent excursion boats (summer only).

Ágios Efstrátios

One of Greece's genuinely remote islands where political prisoners used to be exiled, Ágios Efstrátios lies almost exactly in the centre of the northeast Aegean. Empty horizons on all sides add to the sense of isolation. Its sole village

was built to rehouse islanders after an earthquake in 1967, and owners of its identical houses have gradually added individual touches: flowers, vine arbours, and other features. The harbour is so small that large ferries cannot dock, and passengers are taken ashore by dinghy. There are small swimming coves on the east coast.
40km south of Límnos, served by ferries between Límnos and Rafína on the mainland.

Anáfi

Saucepan-shaped Anáfi has steep sea-cliffs, a high and arid hinterland, around 300 inhabitants, and no cars. Almost all the islanders live in the small port of Ágios Nikólaos, on the south coast, or in Chóra, on the hill immediately above it. Anáfi's beach is at Klisidhi, on the south coast, half an hour's walk from Ágios Nikólaos.
One hour east of Santoríni; infrequent ferries.

Chálki (Khalki)

Like its neighbours Sými and Tílos (*see pp154–5*), Khalki belongs to the southern Dodecanese, is within easy range of Rhodes with its big resorts and international airport, and has become a resort island in its own right. Its harbour village, Emporeió, is very pretty, with fine old houses. Some of these delightful three-storey mansions, with their peeling stucco façades and drooping balconies, are being restored as guesthouses, but many are tumbledown.
50km from Rhodes. Daily ferries (from Kámeiros Skála); frequent hydrofoils (from Rhodes Town).

Khorio

Chálki's medieval village is now a ghost-town, with a dilapidated watchtower of the Knights of St John on a crag above. The walk is rewarded by a fine view of the east coast of Rhodes (*see pp104–5*).
3km west of Emporeió.

Leipsoí's hillsides are dotted with blue-domed churches

Foúrnoi

This barren, hilly island with its scalloped coastline is named after the old-fashioned outdoor bread ovens (*foúrni*), still used in a few villages, which its twin hills resemble from a distance. Its small, peaceful harbour village is spectacularly sited on a glorious west-facing bay, and there are sandy swimming coves, reached by donkey tracks, around its coasts.
18km east of Ikaría, served by frequent Píreas-Ikaría-Sámos ferries.

Kastellórizon (Megísti)

Greece's most remote island lies within a few hundred metres of the Turkish coast. In the 19th century, it was an important trading port, but it went into a decline after its seizure by Italy in 1912. Before World War II, its harbour was a stop on Italian and French flying-boat routes to the Middle East. The war put the seal on the island's decline. From 16,000 people a century ago, there are only 200 now. Despite its ghost-town atmosphere and lack of beaches, it is a delightful island, with fantastic snorkelling around its rocky shores.
105km east of Rhodes; infrequent ferries and infrequent flights from Rhodes.

Koufonísi

The Koufonísi are four inhabited islands, surrounded by several more deserted isles, lying south of Náxos.

Donoússa

Solitude is the only real attraction of this near-deserted island, and with more people seeking it each year it is an increasingly scarce commodity. The population of the only village is less than 100, and facilities for visitors are very primitive.
60km east of Náxos Town.
Infrequent ferries.

Irákleia

The biggest of the Koufonísi offers a choice of places to swim, a harbour-village set on a scenic, fiord-like bay, and walks over rough hillsides to Panagía, its deserted medieval Chóra.
25km south of Náxos Town. Daily ferries.

Koufonísi

Most popular of the group because of the long sandy beach at Finikas, Ano Koufonísia boasts a thriving small fishing fleet berthed in the best natural harbour of the group. There are spectacular sunsets over the bay and the mountains of Náxos.
35km southeast of Náxos Town. Daily ferries in summer.

Schoinoússa

Like Donoússa, Schoinoússa is for those in search of peace and quiet, and as on Donoússa, more arrive each year, overstretching the island's ability to cater for them.
30km southeast of Náxos Town.
Daily ferries.

Psará

Rocky, eerie Psará has a special place in the hearts of Greeks. During the War of Independence, this tiny northeast Aegean isle added its fleet of armed merchant ships to the rebel Greek fleet. In 1824, the Turks landed and massacred most of its inhabitants. The few survivors left the island, which then remained uninhabited from 1824–1834. Even today, its population numbers a mere 460 islanders. There is a choice of beaches, with solitude guaranteed. The view from the small private hotel at the top of the cliff (*tel (0274) 61293*) is truly spectacular.

56km west of Chíos Town, from where a ferry runs four times a week.

Watching the sea go by from a jetty on one of the islands

Sponges are a popular island souvenir

Sými

Tiny Sými retains its delightful serenity, despite a daily invasion of excursionists from Rhodes. In the evening, the island reverts to its natural calm.

27km northwest of Rhodes Town.

Moní Panormítis (Panormítis Monastery)

The 18th-century monastery has a striking carved icon in its small chapel and a mock-Baroque campanile dating from 1905.

15km south of Yialos. Open: daily 8am–1pm & 5–8pm. Donation expected.

Pédion

Pédion is situated on a horseshoe-shaped bay with a sandy bottom and warm water. It is popular with visiting yachts, and its pebbly, tree-lined beach is upgraded each summer with imported truckloads of sand.

2km east of Yialos on the north coast.

Yialos

Yialos is a ghost town with a pleasant air of faded elegance. Around its deep harbour are ranks of tall, elegantly proportioned Neo-Classical mansions. Most are mere shells, but many are now being restored, as is the row of windmills above the harbour.

Boatbuilding still goes on at the small yard on the bay.

North coast of Sými.

Tílos

Blessed with plentiful springs, Tílos abounds with small, fertile valleys and patches of farmland which relieve the barren scenery of its hills.
65km west of Rhodes Town.

Livádia

The main village on the island is a pleasant settlement, half hidden by greenery. On a wide, hill-girt bay, it has a long, pebbly beach.
East coast of Tílos.

Megalo Khorió

This hilltop village overlooks a patchwork of green cultivation. A battlemented fortress of the Knights of St John lends historic interest. Satellite watchtowers of this fortress are scattered somewhat incongruously on lookout hills around the island.
7km northwest of Livádia. Fortress and watchtowers freely accessible.

Mikro Khorió

Deserted since the 1950s, this ghost village makes a fine destination for a lovely walk from Livádia, with rewarding views from its castle keep.
2km west of Livádia.
Castle: free admission.

Typical whitewashed island residences follow the sloping hillsides of Sými

There is something special about dolphins. In ancient times, they were regarded as sacred to the god Apollo, and often appeared in frescoes and on pottery. Today, Greek islanders, like most practical-minded farming people, are not great animal lovers, but when dolphins are spotted from the deck of an island ferry everybody rushes to look. In fact, one of the highlights of any Greek sea journey is the chance of spotting a school of dolphins in the distance or, even better, playing around the ship. The effortless ease with which even young dolphins outpace fast modern ferries is astonishing.

You are most likely to spot dolphins on calm days, when their distinctive, curved dorsal fins can be seen lazily breaking the surface a long way off.

Sadly, as with all Mediterranean sealife, dolphin numbers are dwindling. Heavy pollution from mainland cities – not only in Greece but in Turkey and the Middle East – threatens their environment, and they are also often accidentally taken in the nets of larger fishing vessels in Turkish waters.

Even more at risk is the Mediterranean monk seal (*Monachus monachus*), now down to 400 individuals living and breeding in sea caves on remote islets in the northern Sporádes, the Ionian, Cyclades, and Dodecanese. Growing up to 3m long, it feeds on fish, octopus, and squid. Sensitive and shy, it gives birth, usually to only one pup, every one or two years.

Intensive fishing has reduced the monk seal's food supply, and oil spills

and other forms of pollution also harm them. Rubbish in the water is a growing problem for seals and all other Aegean sealife, and tourism is largely to blame. Tourism is to blame, too, for rapid development and disturbance of remote coastal zones.

HOW TO HELP

1. Don't chase or approach seals if you see them. Don't go on excursions into sea caves where you will disturb them.
2. Discuss your concern about the survival of the monk seal with fishermen and other local people.
3. Report any illegal activities at sea – such as dynamite fishing, spear-fishing with scuba gear, or spear-fishing at night – to port authorities.

Dolphins, whose popularity goes back hundreds of years, as the fresco at Knosós, Crete (above) shows, and the Mediterranean monk seal may be spotted, if you are lucky

Shopping

There are bargains to be found, though perhaps not where you would expect. Souvenir shops in resorts from Corfu to Rhodes sell much the same range of slogan T-shirts and brightly coloured imported leisurewear. For more authentic mementoes of your trip, look in the *laiki* – the municipal street market in larger island villages and towns – for items such as brass goat bells, shepherds' wooden walking sticks, or tiny Greek coffee cups.

Fabric to tempt even the most reluctant shopper

Contrary to popular tourist belief, haggling over prices is not the norm, though the price of everything does drop outside peak tourist season.

Shops traditionally open between 8am and 1pm, close until around 5pm, and re-open until about 8pm, though in major resorts, many shops catering to tourists stay open all afternoon and late into the night. Most shops, except those in resort areas, close on Sunday.

Antiquities and Imitations

You need an export permit to take real antiques or icons out of Greece. This is rarely granted, and genuine antiquities are, in any case, very scarce. Beware of fakes, as they are so well made that it is hard to distinguish them from originals. Archaeological museums in Greece license a range of accurate and attractive replicas, for example of the enigmatic statues of the Cycladic civilisation, that are a much better buy.

Beads and Bangles

Brightly coloured ceramic beads, necklaces, gold- and silver-plated bracelets, and the black and blue glass beads traditionally believed to ward off evil make cheap and cheerful gifts. *Komboloi* or 'worry-beads', carried by many island men, are sold very cheaply at street kiosks and in souvenir shops.

Clothing

Good buys include cotton-knit sweaters and, on more fashionable islands such as Mýkonos, Thíra (Santoríni), or Páros, a wide range of attractive and imaginative summerwear by young Greek designers. Cotton and linen prints, silks, and cotton knits are popular.

Footwear

Boots and shoes are well-made and affordable. In markets on Crete you will find old-fashioned cobblers selling Cretan riding boots. Sandals sold in tourist markets rarely wear well, but on Skýros you can buy the unique, hard-wearing sandals worn by islanders, which are soled with slices of old car tyre. Main street stores in Rhodes Town are a good bet for classic leather shoes at prices well below the European average.

Jewellery

Jewellers abound in small island towns as well as in big resorts. Traditional designs include a variety of good-luck charms, while on Mýkonos, Páros, Náxos, Thíra (Santoríni), and other islands you will find craftsmen working to both modern interpretations and ancient designs. Silver jewellery is cheaper, but gold can be more expensive than elsewhere in Europe.

Lace and Embroidery

Traditionally made lace napkins and tablecloths are excellent buys in Corfu Town and in Rhodes, but beware of cheap, machine-made imitations.

Leather Goods

Leather handbags, satchels, and travel bags made solely for the tourist market are sold in markets wherever holiday-makers go. Prices are low, and this is one area where you may haggle. Workmanship is not always first-rate. Examine seams and straps before buying.

Tax-free Shopping

Value added tax at 18 per cent is charged on anything you buy. Tax-free shopping is available to visitors from outside the European Union at selected shops in the most popular holiday isles. A full list of shops offering VAT refunds to non-EU residents is available from: Tax Free Club, Customer Service Office, Nikis 10, 105 63 Athens (*tel: (01) 3225 569/ 3240 802*). The Hellenic Duty Free Shops chain operates duty-free shops for passengers to non-EU destinations leaving Greece from airports at Chaniá, Corfu, Irakleío, Kós, Mýkonos, Rhodes, Sámos, Santoríni, Skíathos, and Zákynthos.

Lace, embroidery, and striped woollen blankets are good buys on Crete

MARKETS

The local *laiki* market in large island towns sells produce, hardware, and everyday goods, and, with piles of vivid fruit and vegetables, it offers lots of photo opportunities and an insight into local lifestyles, as well as a chance to buy quirky mementoes of your trip.

The *laiki* takes place on weekday mornings and is a great place to stock up on fresh fruit, cheeses, and vegetables for picnics or for self-catering. Here, too, you'll find longer-lasting island specialities such as dried and candied fruit, nuts, sunflower and pumpkin seeds, island honey, and aromatic herbs. Hours vary seasonally: ask for local times at the *dhimotikon* (town hall), island tourist office, or at your hotel.

More formal shopping is patchy and depends very much on the island's holiday clientele: fashionable islands such as Mýkonos have designer boutiques and jewellers to compare with the best in Europe; smaller, simpler islands have smaller, simpler shops.

The best island markets for shopping

Buy fresh *fruit* and vegetables at the *laiki*

and picture-taking are listed here, together with a sample of other shops.

CORFU

Jewellery in silver and in 18- and 20- to 22-carat gold can be found in a row of quality jewellers along the Liston arcades behind the Spianada (*see p32*). A fine choice of island handicrafts is on sale at the National Welfare Organisation shop in The Village, the reconstructed traditional village 8km northwest of Corfu Town.

CRETE
Irakleío

Crete's capital has a fine produce market on Odós 1866. Look for great bundles of oregano and sage, strings of garlic, and the unique corkscrew-like walking sticks made of Cretan dwarf elm favoured by island shepherds.

Chaniá

Chaniá's market area spreads throughout the old quarter, east of Odós Halidhon, and is a mix of shops for locals and tourists. A good place to shop for Cretan boots, and well-made leather bags and satchels.

Réthymno

Colourful and lively market stalls and shops which spill out on to the streets around Porta Guora and Odós Ethnikis Antistasis. Look for souvenirs such as goat bells or Cretan shepherds' daggers.

CHÍOS
Erytha Gift Shop

Pottery, jewellery, and icons inspired by ancient Minoan and Byzantine art.
Hotel Erytha, Karfas.
Tel: (0271) 32311.

Freshly-caught fish for sale

LÉSVOS

Odós Ermou, which runs north–south behind the Mytilíni waterfront as far as the castle walls (*see pp118–19*), is lined with dusty antique shops selling everything from rusting scimitars and flintlock pistols, to tarnished brass and silverware, and engravings of island scenes. It's a great street to browse in. In Mólivos, you'll find a number of imaginative souvenir stores.

Platani
Gold and silver jewellery.
Mólivos. Tel: (0253) 71356.

Renata Hoffmann
Original hand-painted silks.
Mytilíni 9, Mólivos.

PÁROS

Evangelos Skaramagkas
Finely worked and imaginative gold and silverware.
Kástrou, Paroikia. Tel: (0284) 22376.

PÁTMOS

Katoi
Authentic Byzantine icons, ceramics, and sterling silver jewellery.
Chóra. Tel: (0247) 31487.

RHODES

Odós Sokrátous, the shopping thoroughfare of the Old Town (*see pp106–7*), is packed with fine jewellery and leatherware stores. More jewellers plus excellent shoe stores and designer boutiques are to be found on and around Odós Venizelou, in the heart of the New Town. Lambraki, in the New Town, is also a good bet for designer wear.

Babis Ceramics
Original hand-painted ceramics of excellent quality.
Next to Hotel Paradise, Kallithéa. Tel: (0241) 62906.

Dias
Silks and international designer wear.
Dilberaki 16. Tel: (0241) 86153.

Louis Feraud Boutique
International designer clothes.
Lambraki 39. Tel: (0241) 35451.

Rodos Gold
Gold jewellery direct from the factory.
10km south on Líndos Rd. Tel: (0241) 65609.

Romani
Designer fashion accessories and perfumes.
Lambraki 50. Tel: (0241) 27451.

SÝMI

Chouchi Gold
Attractive gold and silver jewellery at bargain prices.
Yialos. Tel: (0241) 71793.

Entertainment

Entertainment in the Greek islands embraces everything from traditional festivals, folk music, and dance, to modern ballet, experimental theatre, and live performances by international artists in every musical field from Bach and Beethoven to rock and roll.

Dancing outside a taverna in Corfu

Many islands host month-long summer art festivals at which the best of Greek artists and international guest performers can be seen and heard, and which offer excellent value for money.

Often these take place within the walls of medieval fortresses or on the stages of 2,000-year-old open-air theatres whose acoustics are still as startlingly clear as when they were built.

The daily English-language *Athens News* and the weekly *Greek News*, which are available from news-stands on most resort islands, list upcoming festivals and other performances on their events pages.

The Greek National Tourist Office also provides lists of events planned for each year, and information on times, ticket prices, and reservations is listed locally by island tourist offices (*see p188-9*). The free *Summertime* listings magazines published for many islands are another useful source of information. (A&P Publishing, Skoufou 10, 105 57 Athens. *Tel: (01) 3226 600.*)

Cinemas

A few larger island towns have cinemas, usually old-fashioned and often open-air, where you can catch recently released US and European films with the original soundtrack and Greek subtitles. Posters around town and outside the cinema will tell you what's on and what's on the way.

Cultural Events

Annual cultural events usually take place in July to September, and may include modern and ancient drama, classical and ethnic music and dance.

ITHÁKI
Itháki Music Contest and Theatre Competition
July
Modern Greek playwrights and composers present their work.
Municipality of Itháki. Tel: (0674) 32795.

LÉSVOS
Jul–Aug
Summer programme of drama and Greek musical performances in the medieval castles at Mólivos and Mytilíni.
Tourist Office for the North Aegean, North Aegean Building, Mytilíni, Lésvos. Tel: (0251) 42511/42513.

SKÍATHOS
Aegean Festival
Aug–Sep
Festival of music and dance, held for the

first time in 1994, featuring Greek and international performers.
Bourtzi Theatre, Skíathos.
Tel: (0427) 23717.

Thásos
Philippi and Thásos Festival
Jul–Aug
Combined programme of dramatic performances held in the ancient theatre at Limin (*see pp126–7*) and at Philippi on the mainland.
Limin, Thásos (Municipality of Thásos).
Tel: (0593) 64004.

Thíra (Santoríni)
International Thíra (Santoríni) Festival
Aug–Sep
Festival of music and arts held in a modern venue in the island's picturesque capital.
Nomicos Convention Centre, Thíra, Santoríni.

Dancing
Luxuries such as television, video, and hi-fi equipment are relatively new to many islands, and islanders, young and old, have not lost the habit of making their own amusement. Even in discos patronised by smart young things from Athens, an evening spent dancing to the latest electronic beat may well end in the small hours with a traditional *sirtos.*

You can sample an evening of the kind of traditional entertainment island Greeks enjoy at any *exoxiko kentro* ('country centre'). These are usually some distance from the town or village, and their clientele is often made up of holidaying Greek expatriates enjoying a nostalgic evening.

One of the best places to see traditional island dances is in Rhodes, where the Nelly Dimoglou troupe of dancers performs at the Ancient Theatre of Rhodes (*tel: (0241) 20157*) every night from May to October.

The Nelly Dimoglou Company of Rhodes keeps traditional dances alive

Discos

Tourism has combined with the Greek love of dancing to ensure that every island resort has an oversupply of discos and dance clubs. Even tiny villages may have two or three discos, often in the open air. These start to warm up well after midnight and play an eclectic mix of the latest international dance hits and rock oldies, often staying open until dawn in defiance of a patchily enforced rule that they should close at 2am. Many are no more than a dance floor, bar, and sound system overlooking the beach, and many survive no more than one or two summers before re-opening under a different guise with a different management and DJ. It is therefore difficult to make hard and fast recommendations, and the venues listed are just a sample.

In any case, there is little to choose between them, except for the DJ's taste in tracks. Admission is usually free, but drinks are two to three times as expensive as in an ordinary bar.

Islands with a long-standing name for bop-till-you-drop nightlife include Corfu, Íos, Páros, and Mýkonos, but it is a quiet island indeed that does not have a nightspot and dance venue.

Dance clubs and nightspots are a popular feature in every village

CORFU (Corfu Town)
Coca Club
Loud, techno dance music.
Ethnikis Antistasseos, Kerkyra.
Sax
Laid-back club, trance music, garden.
Ethnikis Antistasseos, Kerkyra.

ÍOS (Chóra)
Íos Club
Dance music from sunset until dawn.

MÝKONOS (Mýkonos Town)
Anemous
On the town's busiest after-dark street, plays Greek and foreign hits.
Odos Matogiannis, Mýkonos.
Cavo Paradissos
All-night dance club.
Paradissi, Mýkonos.

PÁROS (Paroikia)
Páros caters to a cosmopolitan clientele, with the **Downunder Australian Bar**, **Dubliner Irish Bar**, and **Hard Rock Café** all in the same building, 150m inland at the south end of the esplanade, Akti Vasileou. The **Sodoma Club disco**, and **Opera Club disco** (admission charge) are at the north end of the same street.

RHODES (Rhodes New Town)
Garage
13 Iroon Politechniou.
La Scala
2km south of town centre, next to Rodós Palace Hotel.
Obsession
Panagou Shopping Centre, New Town, Rhodes.

SKÍATHOS (Skíathos Town)
Bourtzoi
Housed in a former olive press, this is the most popular nightspot in town. *Papadiamanti, Skíathos.*

Festivals
Religious festivals in the Greek islands combine solemn ritual with merry-making, feasting, drinking, and dancing. The most important events of the island year are also times of family reunion, when sons and daughters who have emigrated return to their island village. Most of the celebrating takes place the night before the holy day itself.

Easter
This is celebrated according to the Orthodox calendar throughout Greece, with feasting on lamb and goat, usually barbecued outdoors, on Easter Sunday, followed by midnight mass.

Panayiria (Assumption of the Virgin)
15 August
Celebrated on all islands with feasting and dancing. Special pilgrimages and processions are held at Markopoulo on Kefalloniá, on Skíathos, and (the most popular and crowed one) on Tínos.

Sound and Light Shows
CORFU TOWN
Palaio Frourio *15 May–30 Sep*
Times and reservations from Corfu tourist office, New Fortress Square.
Tel: (0661) 37520.

RHODES TOWN
Palace of the Grand Masters *Apr–Oct*
Times and reservations from Rhodes tourist office, corner of Arch Makariou and Papagou. Tel: (0241) 23655.

Television and Video
The television is a fixture in every small island *kafeneon* or taverna. The national TV channels ET1 and ET2 broadcast a steady diet of imported British and US programmes subtitled in Greek. Satellite TV is offered by many larger resort hotels. Many hotels and bars in the more popular island resorts also offer a nightly programme of video movies, sports, and music programmes.

Corfu Ski Club Festival

Children

The Greek islands and their people welcome children warmly, and there are very few places where they cannot be taken. Couples will often be cross-examined: do you have children? If not, why not?

Sand enough for even the most elaborate castle

Islanders regard children as an unmixed blessing, and crying babies or the fractious late-night behaviour of tired youngsters will be tolerated in village *tavernas* and cafés. Above all, life in the Greek islands is lived outdoors almost all year round, and island youngsters are raised on a free-range basis, with the whole village and its surroundings as a playground. Visiting toddlers can easily join in.

Greece welcomes youngsters warmly

Food

Food should not be a problem, even if your children are picky eaters who insist on a chips-only diet. These are on every island menu, as are other plain and familiar dishes such as fish and burgers.

Canned soft drinks are universally available, as are most well-known brands of sweets and chocolate bars, ice cream and ice lollies. Sticky cakes and sweet things from the *zakharoplasteion* (pastry shop) are also a hit with young children.

The Seaside

The main attraction for families visiting the islands is the beach, and sea and sand are the focus of most family resorts. Greek seas have virtually no tide, so the sea is always at your doorstep, and is usually calm enough even for young children to swim in safety. Sheltered, gently shelving, sandy beaches suitable for families with small children can be found on many islands.

Things to Do

Children with an interest in wild flowers and wildlife will find the Greek islands a delight, with dozens of birds, lizards, tortoises, butterflies, and other insects to identify and watch. Those with an interest in marine life will find the clear

Island children spend most of their time outdoors

waters of inlets and harbours as full of sea creatures as any marine aquarium, and will be fascinated by the varied haul unloaded by fishing boats each morning.

The end of any island pier always attracts a gaggle of junior anglers, and simple hook-and-line kits are sold in all village shops.

Pedaloes, canoes, and other simple watersports equipment are for hire at all summer beach resorts, and older children can use them with confidence in shallow waters and enclosed coves. Although island waters have very little tide, they do have strong inshore currents, so caution must be used. Bicycles for children and adults can also be rented at some resorts, and donkey-trekking into the hills is offered on several islands, including Amorgós, Corfu, and Lésvos.

Children with an interest in history will find that ancient sites, medieval castles, and deserted fortresses on almost every island offer a fascinating 'hands-on' lesson in the past, and younger children will enjoy scrambling to the highest tiers of the ancient theatres.

In the unlikely event of poor weather, a visit to one of the many island folklore museums with their displays of traditional costumes, kitchenware, tools, weapons, and jewellery will help to keep children entertained.

Purpose-built facilities and entertain-ment for children are rarely provided in the Greek islands. Many villages have small playgrounds, though their old-fashioned wood and metal swings and roundabouts, and rough gravel are potential hazards for smaller children.

Some larger resorts, hotels, and apartment complexes have separate swimming pools for toddlers, and many package tour operators offer 'fun-clubs', child-minding, and babysitting services (*see* Practical Guide, *p181*).

Sport and Leisure

The great sporting passions of Greece are basketball and football, which islanders play enthusiastically on the dusty village pitch and watch avidly on television. Greece's top teams are on the mainland, in Athens and Thessaloníki. You will see graffiti acclaiming them all over the islands.

Parasailing at Dassia, Corfu

Basketball
Greek Basketball Federation
N Saripolou 11, Athens.
Tel: (01) 8244 125.

Soccer
Major league matches are played regularly on Sundays at 5.30pm in season (October to April). Tickets are available at each team office.
Greek Soccer Federation
Syngrou 137, Athens. Tel: (01) 9336 410.

Golf
The Greek islands offer an ideal climate for golf, with March to November considered the best months. Many new golf courses are under construction.
Corfu Golf Club
18-hole, par-72 course designed by Donald Harradine.
At Ropa, 17km from Corfu Town.
Tel: (0661) 94220.
Afandou Golf Club
19km from Rhodes Town.
Tel: (0241) 51255.

Tennis
Corfu, Crete, and Rhodes are the islands best provided with tennis courts. Many major resorts have their own courts. For further information, contact:

EFOA (Greek Tennis Association)
Omirou 8, Athens. Tel: (01) 8814 916/7.

Trekking and Walking
The Greek islands are wonderful walking country, offering relatively gentle routes for a day's strolling or much more demanding itineraries lasting one or more days. The Levká Óri (White Mountains) of southwest Crete offer some of the most demanding and rewarding trekking in Europe, through landscapes of savage grandeur. On Samothráki, 1,600-m Mount Fengári can be climbed in one full day. Corfu's Pantokrátor region offers gentler walking. Sámos offers trekking in strongly contrasting landscapes, from green woodland to the bare peak of Mount Kerkis, while of the smaller isles, Nísyros, Tílos, and Amorgós offer less demanding hikes.

The Hellenic Alpine Club, which manages refuges in the Cretan mountains, publishes a range of guides and maps, and offers useful advice.

Basic mountain safety rules must be obeyed even on shorter walks, especially in the mountains of Crete, as these and many other places are thinly populated and a sprained ankle far from help could spell disaster. Take plenty of water and make sure that someone knows where you are going and when to expect your return. Proper walking boots, not just trainers, are essential for tougher treks. Other essentials include a water bottle and water sterilising tablets.

Ellinikos Oreivatikos Sindhesmos /EOS (Hellenic Alpine Club)
Karageorgis Servias 7, Athens.
Tel: (01) 3234 555.

WATERSPORTS
Scuba Diving
The seas of Greece offer wonderful diving, with excellent visibility. However, because of the risk of theft from underwater archaeological sites, strict rules apply and diving is permitted only in certain areas. Removing or even photographing any antiquities you find is banned, as is spearfishing with scuba gear if close to a beach.

Diving centres in Greece include:

Calypso Diving Centre
Marasli 24, Ágios Gordis, Corfu.
Tel: (0661) 53101.

International Diving Club
Ornos Beach, Mýkonos.
Tel: (0289) 23220.

Kallithéa Diving School
PO Box 409, Rhodes.
Tel: (0241) 21690.

Diving is also permitted off **Paxos** and **Zákynthos**.

Waterskiing
Waterskiing facilities are available at all holiday beaches in summer, and there are waterski schools at most major resorts. For further information contact:

Greek Waterskiing Association
Stournara 32, Athens. Tel: (01) 5231 875.

Windsurfing
Greek island waters, with their reliable breezes, are perfect for windsurfing, and boards are available for hire at any sizeable resort. A number of international events are held each year.

The west coast of Kós and the bay of Nydrí on Lefkáda are rated among the best windsurfing spots in the Mediterranean.

Greek waters offer great windsurfing conditions

Food and Drink

The best island food is the simplest: fish straight from the boat, and vegetables fresh from the field, served as salad with wild herbs and olives or in stews.

Strings of sun-dried tomatoes

What to Eat

Most resort restaurants offer multilingual menus; where they don't, you will be invited into the kitchen to choose from the pots simmering on the stove. Translations can be puzzling, inviting you to sample 'smashed bowels in roasted spit' or 'one brain salad'. Puzzling them out is half the fun. Food is very often better in smaller, unsophisticated island villages than in bigger resorts, where pressure of numbers forces restaurateurs to fall back on the freezer and the microwave. In a little, family-run pier-side taverna off the beaten track the menu will be much more limited, but the fish will be fresher. Few islanders, even in more sophisticated resorts, are trained chefs, and attempts to serve 'international

Fresh vegetables are preferred to canned or frozen products

cuisine' are almost always less successful than the basic dishes of the islands.

Only in the smartest restaurants will food be served course by course. *Meze*, which is a selection of dishes served simultaneously, is a Greek culinary tradition, and in smaller places everything comes at once or in an unexpected order – chips, for example, often arrive as an appetizer.

Islanders, like all Greeks, tend to eat late when they eat out, and a restaurant which seemed empty when you sat down to dinner is often full of diners by the time you are ready to leave.

Fish

Fish is priced according to weight and category. You choose your fish from the kitchen, where it is weighed and the price is calculated before filleting. Seafood is popular but more expensive every year, with delicacies such as *barbounia* (red mullet) and *melanouryia* (blacktail) at the top of the price range. Swordfish (*xifias*) steaks are always available and moderately priced, usually coming in enormous portions. At the cheaper end of the scale are *marides* (whitebait), *goupes* (sprats), and *kalamares* (fried, battered baby squid). *Astakos* (langouste, though usually translated as lobster) is expensive by local standards, though most visitors will think it good value. Unfamiliar seafood dishes include *oktapodhi* (octopus), served in a variety of ways, either cold as a snack, grilled, or in a stew (*stifadho*) with rice or pasta.

Meat Dishes

Moussaka (lamb or veal cooked in layers of white sauce, cheese, and aubergine, or sometimes potato), *yiouvetsi/pastitsio* (beef stewed with noodles in a clay pot), *kotopoulo* (roast or grilled chicken), and *souvlaki* (pork, veal, or lamb cooked on a skewer) appear on most menus, as do *kefthedhes* (meat balls in sauce), *paidakia* (lamb chops), and *brisoles* (pork or veal cutlets).

Vegetable Dishes

The traditional Greek salad is a meal in itself, and few restaurants will mind if you order it and nothing else. It is basically a great heap of tomatoes, onion, cucumber, green peppers, and olives, sprinkled with dried oregano. It is known as *horiatiki* ('village salad') only in tourist restaurants, where it is usually served crowned with feta cheese (if you don't want the cheese, ask for *salata horeis feta*, salad without feta).

Dishes such as *gemista* (tomatoes or green peppers stuffed with herb-flavoured rice) and *dolmades* (stuffed vine leaves) may or may not contain meat. Vegetable-only dishes include *vriam* (ratatouille), a variety of pulses including *fakes* (lentil stew), *gigantes* (stewed broad beans), *mavromati* (boiled black-eye beans served cold with coriander), and *fasolakia* (green beans stewed with tomatoes). Cold dishes include *tsatsiki* (yoghurt flavoured with cucumber and garlic).

Chips are a favoured side serving with meat dishes.

If you do not eat meat, try telling the restaurateur that you are a *hortophagos* – a vegetarian.

Octopus is a famed island delicacy

What to Drink

Beer

Almost all beers sold in Greece are strong lagers, brewed locally under licence and always served ice-cold. Common brands include Amstel, Beck's, Henninger, Heineken, Kaiser, and Kronenbourg, all around 5 per cent alcohol by volume and usually sold in 550ml bottles. Imported beers such as Sol and Corona are often sold in smarter bars; British brands such as Newcastle Brown Ale, along with Irish Guinness, are also found in island resorts with a British clientele.

Prices vary widely and largely depend on where you drink, not what you drink. A small bottle of imported beer in a neon-lit cocktail bar may cost three times as much as a large bottle in a local taverna.

Brandy

Locally made brandy – sometimes described as *koniak* (cognac) – comes in three-, five-, and seven-star quality. Sweeter than French brandies, it makes a pleasant after-dinner drink. Best-known brands include Metaxa, Cambas, and Sámos.

Coffee and Tea

Kafes ellinikos (Greek coffee) comes black and thick, in thimble-sized cups, and is always served with a glass of water. Don't stir it or you will disturb the grounds, which are left in the cup. If you like it without sugar ask for *sketo*; if you like extra sugar ask for *gliko*. Most Greeks drink it *metrio*, with one measure of sugar. Instant coffee, whatever the brand, is called Nes and is

Greek wines are very affordable

often served iced (*frappé*). *Tsai* (tea) is available almost everywhere and is invariably made with Lipton's tea bags. If you like your tea or coffee with milk, ask for it *me gala*.

Imported and Local Spirits

Imported liquors such as Scotch, bourbon, vodka, and gin generally cost a lot more than the local spirits, and are mostly destined only to be cocktail ingredients. Measures, however, are always generous.

Ouzo

Sunset is the customary time to take your Greek aperitif, though *ouzo* is drunk at any hour. A clear, sweet, aniseed-flavoured spirit, it is always served with a glass of water and usually with ice. It turns cloudy when water is added. *Ouzo* from Lésvos and Chíos is highly thought of.

Retsina

Retsina (a resinated wine) was formerly stored in earthenware jugs proofed with pine resin, which gave it a distinctive flavour. Today, resin is added artificially. It is an acquired taste, but one worth acquiring quickly, as it is by far the cheapest of Greek wines.

In many island villages the taverna will sell *retsina apo to bareli* (from the barrel), and sampling it is always an experience. Whatever you really think, be sure to praise it extravagantly – the landlord may have made it himself!

Soft Drinks

All the well-known brands are available on every island, as are various fruit juices sold by the carton. Freshly squeezed orange juice, available in pricier cafés in resorts, is remarkably expensive in a country which grows so many oranges.

Tsipouro

A clear and lethal spirit made (like Italian *grappa*) from the skins and pulp left over after pressing grapes to make wine. You are unlikely to find *tsipouro* in most bars: it's a winter drink, kept for local consumption in the coldest months, January and February.

Wine

The Greek islands produce a choice of red, white, and dessert wines, all of them affordable and few outstanding. Whites are often better than reds. Sámos produces one of the few Greek wines which will stand international comparison: Samaina, a crisp, dry white. The Robola range of red and white wines from Kefalloniá is also highly regarded.

Thíra (Santoríni) produces Santoríni Boutari, a fine, dry white by one of Greece's leading winemakers.

In addition to these the CAIR and Emery wineries of Rhodes produce a very good sparkling white.

Ouzo, Greece's national spirit, comes in many different bottles

Where to Eat

You can eat well in even the smallest of island villages, though the menu may be limited to the catch of the day and whatever fruit and vegetables are in season locally. In most resorts and towns there is little to choose between one eating place and its neighbour, so stroll down the beach or wander around the harbour and pick whichever takes your fancy.

Eat where islanders or holidaying Athenians eat and you will eat better, cheaper, and more varied meals than in restaurants catering only to holidaymakers. For many island restaurants the quality of food is not so important as the setting, the view, the atmosphere, or the ebullient charm of the proprietor.

Below are restaurants listed on the bigger and more popular islands, as well as a handful of other places which stand out from the crowd.

The following table gives an indication of restaurant prices. The star rating indicates the cost of a three-course meal, per person, without wine. A half-litre carafe of *retsina* or a bottle of beer costs around ¤ 1.00, a bottle of red or white wine between ¤ 4.50 and ¤ 6.00.

Very few island restaurants accept telephone reservations (or even have a telephone). Prices are up to 50 per cent higher across the board in international holiday resorts than in backwater island restaurants, and may increase by up to 20 per cent a year, so only a rough price guide can be given. Additionally, many restaurants in island resorts are leased by the year: a restaurant may close in October to re-open next spring under

A Greek salad is a meal on its own

different management with a new image and menu, while the previous manager and chef pop up on a different street, or even on a different island.

★	up to €9.00
★★	€9.00–€13.00
★★★	€13.00–€17.50
★★★★	more than €17.50

CHÍOS
Perivoli ★★★
Excellent local menu, island wines, and Greek dancing every Friday evening.
Argenti 9–11, Kampos, Chíos.
Tel: (0271) 31973.

CORFU
Venetsianiko Pigadhi ★★★
Good Greek food, even more attractive location in a lovely old courtyard.
Plateia Kremasti, Corfu Town.
La Famiglia ★★
Family-run restaurant with an imaginative blend of traditional and modern cooking.
Kantouni tou Vizi, Corfu Town.

CRETE

Thalassino Ageri ★★★
One of Chania's best seafood restaurants, right on the old harbour.
Vivilaki 35, Chania.

Karnagia, Chania ★
Value-for-money courtyard restaurant in the old town, serving Greek food.
Katehaki 8, Chania.

Kyria Maria ★★
Characteristic home-cooked Cretan dishes in this family-run open-air restaurant on a quiet side street.
Moschovitou 20, Réthymno.

KÓS

Most of Kós Town's restaurants and tavernas are along Vasilis Georgiou, the beach esplanade south of the Kástro, or around the harbour on Akti Kountouriouti.

Platanos ★★/★★★
Traditional taverna with Greek dishes, beside the castle and ancient plane tree.
Platía Hippokratous, Kós Town.
Tel: (0242) 28991.

White Tower ★★/★★★
Good grill restaurant.
Akti Kountouriouti 13, Kós town.
Tel: (0242) 22638.

LÉSVOS

Okhtapodhi ('The Octopus') ★★/★★★
The oldest and best of several traditional restaurants on the harbour at Mólivos.
Limenon, Mólivos.

LÍMNOS

Psarotaverna O Glaros ★★★
Excellent seafood restaurant with a fine view of the floodlit Genoese castle.
On the small fishing harbour, 500m east of Platía Oktobriou 8.

MÝKONOS

Katrin's ★★★★
One of the finest and most expensive eating places in the islands, serving up-market Greek and French cuisine.
Chora, Mýkonos.

PÁROS

Apollon ★★★
Garden restaurant with a collection of works by local artists adorning its walls. The menu features island specialities, mostly grilled meat dishes.
Paralia, Parikia.

RHODES

To Steno ★★
This traditional-style *ouzeri* serves snacks, ouzo, Land wine, and offers a good lunch choice.
Aghios Anargyros 29, Rhodes New Town.

Alexis ★★★★
Fine fish and lobster, pleasant Old Town surroundings, but the island's highest prices.
Sokratous 18, Rhodes Old Town.

Deciding what to eat can be a difficult choice

H o t e l s   a n d   A c c o m m o d a t i o n

Finding somewhere to stay is rarely a problem in the Greek islands in summer. There is accommodation to suit all pockets in all but the tiniest villages, where you may find the local shopkeeper is willing to rent a spare room (or, in summer, a camp bed in the garden or on the roof).

Private villas offer luxury and privacy

However, almost all island *pensions* and hotels close in mid-October and do not re-open until April. You should also book well ahead for accommodation at Easter and Panayiria (*see p165*), when millions of expatriate Greeks return to their native islands.

Accommodation is licensed by the government, which classifies hotels, *pensions,* apartments, and privately rented rooms in categories A to E. This national system is based on the services and facilities offered, not on quality, so a drab old hotel with televisions and telephones in the bedrooms and a mediocre restaurant will rate higher than a bright new one without such services. Many attractive new properties have no grading. The system should be treated with caution.

The government grading system does, however, give a guide to prices. In July and August prices can be up to 30 per cent more than in the shoulder-season months. A recently constructed twin room with en-suite facilities costs from around €15 in a small, family-run pension to €150 in a top hotel. A C-class hotel (equivalent to 3-star) will be between €30 and €45 per room.

Apartments

Self-catering apartments on the most popular islands are excellent value for money, especially for families. Most have two bedrooms (or one bedroom and a convertible lounge) and a kitchen with two-ring electric cooker, fridge, crockery, cutlery, and cooking utensils. In high season they are used mainly by package tour companies, but in spring and autumn these apartments are often available at bargain rates to independent travellers.

Campsites

Visitors who have had experience of the generally excellent campsites on the Greek mainland will be disappointed by the poor facilities, dirt, litter, and lack of amenities on most island campsites. Mainly used by young backpackers on a tight budget, they are no bargain.

Hotels

A-class luxury hotels are to be found only on islands which are long-standing favourites, primarily Corfu, Crete (Elounda area), and Rhodes. An exception is the superb Akti Mýrina hotel, a Caribbean-style bungalow complex on the otherwise unexciting island of Límnos (*see p117*): (81400 Límnos. *Tel: (0254) 22681*). There are C-class hotels, usually big, bland, and busy, on every island that has an international airport.

D- and E-class hotels, found in many larger commercial ports, are very cheap but often grubby and run-down. For lone travellers, they offer the advantage of single rooms at lower rates.

Pensions

Small, family-run *pensions*, usually with around a dozen twin-bedded rooms, are excellent value. Most are recently built, with en-suite facilities in rooms and solar-heated water.

Unique Places to Stay

There are many stylish and colourful 'boutique hotels' in the Greek islands, often in architecturally interesting, historic buildings, usually family-run.

You will find many such properties in the Venetian quarters of Chania and Rethymnon on Crete, on the island of Sými, in the lovely clifftop village of Oía on Thíra (Santoríni) (*see pp68–9*), on Hydra in the Argo-Saronic islands (*see p51*), and in the Cycladic islands of Mýkonos (*see pp60–61*), Páros (*see pp66–7*), or Folégandros (*see p56*).

Villas

Luxury villas, some with their own pool and landscaped grounds, can be found on Corfu, Paxoí, and some other islands. Travel agents should have information of those tour operators offering villa packages.

Places to stay include modern resort hotels

On Business

Despite numerous European Union grants and loans, the urgings of the International Monetary Fund, and attempts to modernise and reform, Greece's economy remains the most problematic in the EU.

Joining the European Union heralds a new phase for the economy

Business is burdened by an inefficient, underpaid bureaucracy. Privatisation of the cumbersome, militant public sector has been put on hold.

The breaking up of the former Yugoslavia, Greece's northern neighbour, and the wars in Bosnia and Kosovo have also had a disruptive effect on the economy.

Shipping and tourism compete as Greece's top two foreign currency earners, with agriculture in third place. The shipping industry is in the hands of a relatively small number of private companies, several of which also extend into the tourism sector, but small, family-run operations predominate in farming and tourism.

Many Greek executives have been educated in the US, Britain, and Canada, and almost all speak fluent English and are familiar with the needs of their overseas colleagues. However, a new breed of executive sees Europe, rather than the Anglo-Saxon countries, as its role model, and since joining the European Union, Greece's economy has stepped out of the shadow of the US.

Accommodation

Major hotel chains are thin on the ground on most islands, though Hilton International has a branch in Corfu. Greece's major home-grown hotel groups, Capsis, Chandris, and Astir, have reliable hotels on the more popular resort islands. Elsewhere, hotels are designed primarily for holidaymakers, but offer basic business-traveller requirements such as direct-dial phone facilities in bedrooms. Fax and telex communications can be found on almost all islands. Finding international-standard accommodation anywhere except Corfu, Crete, and Rhodes outside the April to October holiday season poses problems, as most properties close down for winter.

Business Etiquette

Greek business etiquette is relaxed. Punctuality is appreciated, but turning up late for a meeting is not a mortal sin. Normal business-wear is jacket and tie for men (a suit is not essential) and skirt, dress, or trouser suit for women. Not all offices are air-conditioned, and in summer many executives dispense with jacket and tie in favour of open-necked, short-sleeved shirt, and slacks. Many offices close between noon and 4pm, and many business people take an extended holiday from mid-July to late August.

Business Transport

Olympic Airways, Air Greece, Cronus

Airlines, and Axon Air operate an extensive inter-island network. Flights should be reserved before you arrive in Greece, as they are often overbooked. Informally, passengers connecting with international Olympic flights get preference. There are no direct international scheduled flights to the Greek islands from Britain or the USA. Air taxi and helicopter services are available from Athens airport.

Alternative rapid transport to and between islands in summer is the network of high-speed hydrofoils and catamarans.

On the Ground

Taxis are the most convenient way of getting around, and they meet most island flights and ferries. Car rental is available on virtually all islands through international and local companies, but is expensive. Hiring a taxi by the day is a practical alternative.

Communications

Surprisingly, phoning locally or internationally is often easier on smaller islands than it is in Athens: many islands have newer, more recently installed equipment. Operators are usually helpful and competent in English. Fax facilities are widely available, even in out-of-the-way places and family-run hotels. Sending a fax message is often easier and less time-consuming than making a phone call.

Conference and Exhibition Facilities

Several islands offer facilities for conferences and exhibitions. Corfu upgraded its facilities when it hosted an EU summit in 1994, and is a popular meetings and incentive travel destination, as are Rhodes, Crete, and, to a lesser extent, Kós. The best conference and exhibition venues are in major international hotels.

CORFU

Corfu Hilton, Kanoni, Corfu.
Tel: (0661) 36540/9.

CRETE

Elounda Beach Hotel, Elounda, Crete.
Tel: (0841) 41412/3.

KÓS

Neptune Hotels Resort, Mastihari.
Tel: (0242) 41785.

RHODES

Rodos Palace Hotel, Rhodes.
Tel: (0241) 25222/32.

Secretarial and Translation Services

Bilingual secretarial services and translation facilities are not widely available in island hotels or elsewhere.

Media

Two English-language magazines, *Greece's Weekly* and *Odyssey*, are useful sources of information for the business traveller. *Greece's Daily*, a news preview distributed by fax, provides news and analysis ahead of the Greek and international daily press.

Keeping up with events around the world

Practical Guide

Arriving

By Air

There are international airports on Corfu, Crete, Kárpathos, Kefalloniá, Kýthira, Kós, Lésvos, Mýkonos, Rhodes, Sámos, Thíra (Santoríni), Skíathos, and Zákynthos, and these receive charter flights between April and November from most European countries. All scheduled services, however, use Athens or Thessaloníki airports on the Greek mainland, with onward domestic flights which also serve an expanding network including Chíos, Ikaria, Límnos, Léros, Páros, Skýros, Náxos, Kastellórizo, and Kýthira.

Domestic flights are often overbooked. If you plan to fly within Greece, book flights before you leave home and always reconfirm. Facilities at island airports are basic. On most islands, taxis are the only transport to and from the airport for passengers who are not on a package holiday. Car rental companies have desks at most of the larger island airports.

On most islands, buses are timed to meet ferries

By Sea

Many ferry companies ply the Greek island routes, connecting them with each other and with Píreas, the port of Athens. State-of-the-art Greek ferries dominate the Adriatic Sea. Journey times range from under an hour for islands close to the mainland to around 14 hours (from Píreas to Rhodes). Ferries also operate from Thessaloníki, Kavála, and Alexandroúpoli on the northern mainland to the Sporádes and northeast Aegean islands, and from Igoumenítsa and Pátra on the west coast to the Ionian isles. You can also arrive in Greece via Corfu with ferries from the Italian ports of Ancona, Bari, Otranto Venice, and Brindisi; via Crete from Egypt and Israel; and via Rhodes, Kós, Sámos, Chíos, and Lésvos from ports on the nearby Turkish coast. The *Thomas Cook European Timetable* has details of ferry times (*see p187*).

Passports and Visas

Passports are required by all except European Union citizens, who may use national identity cards. British visitors need a full British passport and are allowed a maximum stay of six months. Citizens of the USA, Canada, Australia, and New Zealand may visit for up to three months without a visa, but citizens of South Africa do need a visa. Travellers who require visas should obtain them in their country of residence.

Camping

A list of island campsites is available from the Greek National Tourist Office (*see pp188–9*) and from the Greek Camping Association, Solonos 102, 10680 Athens (*tel: (01) 3621 560*). Camping or sleeping rough on beaches is illegal, a rule which is widely ignored.

Children

There are few special facilities for babies or older children, except where provided for package tour clients. These often include babysitting for younger infants, playgroups for toddlers, and activity groups for younger children. Baby milk, food, and nappies are available at most mini-markets in tourist resorts, and elsewhere from the *geniko emporion* (general store) or from pharmacies.

Climate

Each island has its own climate depending on the winds and sea currents. Generally, winters are mild and short, with rainfall at its highest and temperatures at their lowest in February, around 8–10°C, much colder on the mountains of Crete and anywhere above 1,000m. By March, days are warmer, and April and May are changeable, with warm sunshine but a possibility of rain. It rarely rains between June and late September. Midsummer temperatures average more than 30°C.

Weather Conversion Chart
25.4mm = 1 inch
°F = 1.8 x °C + 32

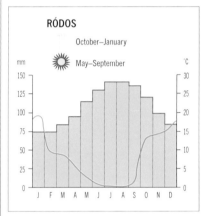

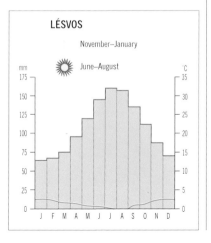

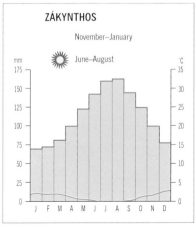

Plenty of motorcycles and mopeds are available for hire

Crime

The islands have very low rates of theft or violent crime against tourists. That said, normal caution should be exercised. Look after money, traveller's cheques, credit cards, and other valuables.

Customs Regulations

Normal EU rules apply. Non-EU visitors may bring in 200 cigarettes, 50 cigars or 250g of tobacco, one litre of spirits, two litres of wine or liqueurs, 50ml of perfume, and 250ml of cologne. It is forbidden to export antiquities and works of art found in Greece.

Driving
Accidents

If possible, set up warning signs. Your hire car should be equipped with a warning triangle, but not all are. If someone is injured, the accident must be reported to the police (*see p184*). Passers-by in such cases are required to stop and assist. Contact the police as a precaution, even if the only damage is to vehicles.

If you can, write down the names and addresses of other drivers involved, the make and licence numbers of vehicles, the names of any witnesses, and the date and time of the accident. If possible, take photographs.

Under no circumstances admit liability, sign any statement of responsibility, or lose your temper.

Breakdown

The Automobile and Touring Club of Greece (ELPA) provides tourist information and road assistance. *Tel: 174* and *104* respectively on all islands except: Corfu (*tel: (0661) 39504*); Crete, Irakleío office (*tel: (0841) 289440*), Chaniá office (*tel: (0821) 26059*). ELPA's coverage of the islands is patchy, but there are competent vehicle repair shops and mechanics in most villages. In the last few years, the company Express Service is gradually overshadowing ELPA.

Car Hire

International chains are represented on all resort islands, with desks in island capitals and at international airports. There are also small local companies on almost every island, but car hire is less expensive if you hire through an international chain before leaving home. Rental cars, even from major chains, can be under-maintained. Check tyres, brakes, steering, spare tyre, and lights before you leave the depot (*also see* Rules of the Road, *p184*). Full collision damage waiver (CDW), personal accident insurance, bail bond, and liability cover are essential. Even international companies often exclude damage to the underside of the vehicle or the tyres from their CDW. Make sure your own insurance covers such damage.

Documentation

A full British or other EU driving licence is valid. Most other nationalities need an international driving licence.

Drink-driving

Penalties are severe and the best advice is to avoid alcohol when driving.

Fines

Police may impose fines for motoring offences on the spot but may not collect them there and then. The fine must be paid at a Public Treasury office or a bank within 10 days.

Fuel

Petrol costs around the European average, with diesel fuel being much cheaper. Lead-free fuel is widely available. It is forbidden to carry fuel in a container in the vehicle. Few petrol stations accept credit cards, and most are not self-service.

Navigation, Maps, and Road Signs

Romanised (conventional Western) spellings of Greek place names vary. However, the names are usually recognisable. On main roads, signs are in the Roman alphabet as well as in Greek. On some routes, there will be no signs. Many new roads are not yet shown on island maps.

Rules of the Road

Speed limits are 50kph in built-up areas, 80kph outside built-up areas, and 120kph on motorways. In practice, much lower speeds than these are advisable on winding and poorly surfaced island roads.

Seatbelts, where fitted, must be worn. You can be fined for not carrying a warning triangle, fire extinguisher, and first aid kit. Many rental cars lack these.

Electricity

Voltage is 220V AC. You may require an adaptor for the round two-pin sockets used in Greece. Power cuts are not uncommon, so take along candles and/or a torch. Appliances using US-style 110V power supply need a step-down transformer and socket adaptor.

Choose from a variety of international and local car rental agencies

Embassies and Consulates
Australia
37 Dimitriou Soutsou, Athens.
Tel: (01) 644 7303.
Canada
Gennadhiou 4, Athens.
Tel: (01) 723 9511.
New Zealand
Represented by UK Consulate.
United Kingdom
Ploutarchou 1, Athens.
Tel: (01) 723 6211/19.
USA
Vassilissis Sofias 91, Athens.
Tel: (01) 7212 951/9 & 7218 400/1.

Emergency Telephone Numbers
Ambulance *166*
General Emergency *100* (manned by the police and dealing with crime, fire, and medical emergencies).
Fire Brigade *199* (Cities and Forests)
Thomas Cook Report loss or theft of Thomas Cook Traveller's Cheques.
Tel: 00 44 1733 318950 (24 hours).

Health
There are no mandatory vaccination requirements, but it is recommended that you have up-to-date immunisations against tetanus and polio, plus hepatitis A and typhoid if you intend to travel to some of the remoter areas. AIDS is present. Food and water are safe.

All EU countries have reciprocal arrangements for reclaiming the cost of medical services. UK residents should obtain form E 111 from any UK post office. Claiming is laborious, and covers only medical care, not secondary examinations (such as X-rays),

By bicycle and boat is a good way to cover the smaller islands

emergency repatriation, and so on. You are advised to take out adequate travel insurance, available through the AA, branches of Thomas Cook, and most travel agents.

Measurements and Sizes
Greece uses standard European measurements and sizes.

Media
The English-language newspapers *Athens News* (daily) and *Greek News* (weekly) give a quirky insight into national news and views. The bi-monthly glossy magazine *Odyssey* takes a more thoughtful approach.

British, US, and European newspapers are on sale in most resort islands 24 to 48 hours after publication. British news bulletins are broadcast on the ERT2 radio station (98KHz) at 2pm and 9pm. The BBC World Service can be received on 9.41, 12.09, and 15.07 MHz.

Money Matters
The Euro (€) is the unit of currency used in the islands. There are seven denominations of the Euro note: €5,

€10, €20, €50, €100, €200, and €500; eight denominations of coins: 1 cent, 2 cents, 5 cents, 10 cents, 20 cents, 50 cents, and €1 and €2. Most major currencies and traveller's cheques can be exchanged at banks, post offices, and travel agencies. The latter charge a higher commission but are open when banks and post offices are shut. Banks and post offices generally open 8am–2pm weekdays only. Credit cards are accepted only in expensive hotels, shops, and some restaurants in more popular resorts. MasterCard and Visa are the most widely accepted.

Thomas Cook MasterCard Traveller's Cheques free you from the hazards of carrying large amounts of cash, and in the event of loss or theft, they can quickly be refunded. Sterling cheques are recommended, though cheques in US dollars are accepted. Large hotels, some shops, ticket and travel agencies, and car rental offices in main resort islands accept traveller's cheques.

The following branches of Thomas Cook can provide emergency assistance in the case of loss or theft of Thomas Cook MasterCard Traveller's Cheques. They can also provide full foreign exchange facilities, and will cash traveller's cheques (free of commission in the case of Thomas Cook MasterCard Traveller's Cheques): Karayeorgias Servis 4, Sindagma, Athens, and Thomas Cook Bureau de Change, Othonos Amalias 25, Pátras.

If you need to transfer money quickly, you can use the MoneyGram℠ Money Transfer service. For more details in the United Kingdom, you can telephone *Freephone 0800 897198.*

Conversion Table

FROM	TO	MULTIPLY BY
Inches	Centimetres	2.54
Feet	Metres	0.3048
Yards	Metres	0.9144
Miles	Kilometres	1.6090
Acres	Hectares	0.4047
Gallons	Litres	4.5460
Ounces	Grams	28.35
Pounds	Grams	453.6
Pounds	Kilograms	0.4536
Tons	Tonnes	1.0160

To convert back, for example from centimetres to inches, divide by the number in the third column.

Men's Suits

UK	36	38	40	42	44	46	48
Rest of Europe	46	48	50	52	54	56	58
US	36	38	40	42	44	46	48

Dress Sizes

UK	8	10	12	14	16	18
France	36	38	40	42	44	46
Italy	38	40	42	44	46	48
Rest of Europe	34	36	38	40	42	44
US	6	8	10	12	14	16

Men's Shirts

UK	14	14.5	15	15.5	16	16.5	17
Rest of Europe	36	37	38	39/40	41	42	43
US	14	14.5	15	15.5	16	16.5	17

Men's Shoes

UK	7	7.5	8.5	9.5	10.5	11
Rest of Europe	41	42	43	44	45	46
US	8	8.5	9.5	10.5	11.5	12

Women's Shoes

UK	4.5	5	5.5	6	6.5	7
Rest of Europe	38	38	39	39	40	41
US	6	6.5	7	7.5	8	8.5

National Holidays

Note that dates for Easter and associated moveable feasts, determined by the Greek Orthodox calendar, can vary from the Christian calendar by up to three weeks.

New Year's Day (1 January)
Epiphany (6 January)
Shrove Monday ('Clean Monday')
Independence Day (25 March)
Good Friday
Easter Sunday and Monday
Labour Day (1 May)
Day of the Holy Spirit (Whit Monday)
Assumption of the Virgin Mary (15 August)
Ochi Day (28 October)
Christmas Day (25 December)
St Stephen's Day (26 December)

Opening Hours

Banks *see* Money Matters on *p185*.

Museums and Sites

Opening hours given by official sources often bear no relation to the hours in force, which may change without notice. Most sites are open 8.30am–3pm, Tuesday to Sunday. Some major sites on Crete stay open longer in summer. Winter hours (November to March) are usually shorter.

Shops

These traditionally open from 8am–1pm, and 5–8pm. Shops catering to tourists stay open longer. Most shops outside main resort areas close on Sunday.

Organised Tours

Organised tours arranged by tour agencies at your resort can be an

Keep in touch

affordable way of exploring the island if you have no transport of your own or are reluctant to drive. Drawbacks include those of travelling with a group.

Pharmacies

A green or red cross marks the *farmakio*. Greek chemists have some medical training, and can advise and prescribe medicines for common ailments. Pharmacies open during normal shop hours from Monday to Friday.

Places of Worship

Sunday services at most Orthodox churches are held from around 7.30am, and last for some hours. Decently dressed visitors (long trousers and shirt sleeves for men, below-the-knee and arm-covering dresses for women) may attend. There are Roman Catholic churches on Tínos and Sýros.

Police

See Emergency Numbers on *p184*.

Postal Services

Most larger island villages have a post office, distinguished by its prominent circular yellow sign. They are normally open weekdays during shop hours, but city-centre post offices are also open on Saturday mornings. It is often quicker to change money at a post office than at a bank. Stamps (*grammatosima*) are also sold at kiosks and postcard shops. Parcels for posting must be inspected by the post office clerk before sealing. Air-mail letters take three to six days to reach the rest of Europe, five to eight days for North America, and slightly longer for Australasia. Cards take much longer.

Public Transport
Island Buses

Buses are the only public transport available on the Greek islands. Frequencies and services are geared to the needs of islanders, not of tourists: buses are cheap, but hot, crowded, and rickety, and do not always serve the sights you want to go to at the time you want to go, if at all. Double-check the destination with the conductor: destination boards often indicate where the bus has come from, not where it is bound. Buy tickets on board.

Ferries

Píreas, the port of Athens, is the main gateway to the Aegean islands. Many nearby islands are served by hydrofoils, some of which go from Zea Marina, about 3km away. Hydrofoils and ferries also go to Évvoia and to the Cyclades from Rafina, about 30km east of Athens. Timetables are published monthly by the Greek National Tourist Office (*see pp188–9*). Many islands are served by ferries from other mainland ports. From mid-June to mid-September inter island connectivity is upgraded to regular daily ferries.

The *Thomas Cook European Timetable* and the Independent Traveller's guide, *Greek Island Hopping* have details of ferry times, and can be obtained from Thomas Cook branches in the UK.

Taxis

Taxis are everyday transport for islanders, and will go virtually anywhere. Fares are metered, and most taxi drivers are friendly, honest, and helpful, though overcharging is common when going to and from airports. Beware, too, in Athens and Píreas, where taxi drivers are notoriously dishonest with tourists.

A green or red cross usually indicates a pharmacy

Senior Citizens

Older visitors accustomed to cooler climes may find the islands pleasanter in April or May, or after mid-September, when temperatures are less scorching. Just as Greeks love children, they respect older people, but age brings no privileges. Older people are expected to fend for themselves; for example, when boarding a bus or ferry. In a country where queuing is unknown, this can be trying.

Telephones

The easiest way to call is from a metered telephone. You pay at the end of the call. Few allow the use of charge cards, reverse-charge (call collect) calls, or incoming calls. Metered phones are also available in booths at OTE (Greek Telecommunications Organisation) offices. You can buy telephone cards from OTE offices, and from many shops and kiosks. This is definitely the cheapest way to call.

In the last few years, OTE has installed thousands of telephone booths on all islands, and the new, fully digitalised network allows easy access to the world.

The Thomas Cook Traveltalk card is an international pre-paid telephone card supported by 24-hour multilingual customer service. Available from Thomas Cook branches in the UK in £10 and £20 denominations, the card can be re-charged by calling the customer service unit, and quoting your credit card number. Dialling codes within Greece for the three major mainland cities are:

Athens: *01*
Pátra: *061*
Thessaloníki: *031*

Thomas Cook

See *p185* for details of Thomas Cook locations in the Greek islands.
Thomas Cook's World Wide Web site, at *www.thomascook.com*, provides up-to-the-minute details of Thomas Cook's travel and foreign money services.

Time

GMT+2 hours (+3 hours in summer). Clocks change in spring and autumn on the same date as other EU countries, but this does not always coincide with non-EU countries.

Tipping

Service is included in restaurants and it is common also to leave small change on the table. This also applies to bars and cafés. There is no pressure to tip in hotels, but it is always welcomed. In taxis, 'keep the change' is normal practice.

Toilets

Standards vary enormously, but there have been dramatic improvements. Toilets in cafés and tavernas are usually better than public facilities. Greek plumbing is easily blocked because of low water pressure, so except in the most modern hotels do not flush toilet paper but put it in the bin provided.

Tourist Information

The Greek National Tourist Office (GNTO) provides a range of information which includes hotel listings, up-to-date transport schedules, and details of sites and events.

GNTO Head Office: 2 Amerikis St,
105 64 Athens. Tel: (01) 327 1300/2;
email: info@gnto.gr

Outside the Greek Islands
Australia
51–7 Pitt Street, Sydney NSW 2000.
Tel: (02) 241 1663.
Canada
1300 Bay Street, Main Level, Toronto,
Ontario M5R 3K8. *Tel: (416) 968 2220.*
1223 Rue de la Montagne, Montreal,
Quebec, H3G 1Z2. *Tel: (514) 871 1535.*
United Kingdom
4 Conduit Street, London W1R 0DJ.
Tel: (020) 7734 5997.
USA
645 Fifth Avenue, New York NY 10022.
Tel: (212) 421 5777.
168 North Michigan Avenue, Chicago
IL 60601. *Tel: (312) 782 1084.*
611 West 6th Street, Suite 2198, Los
Angeles CA 90017. *Tel: (213) 626 6696.*

In the Greek Islands
Corfu
Corfu Tourist Office, New Fortress
Square, Corfu. *Tel: (0661) 37520.*
Crete
Chaniá Information Office, Kriari 40,
731 00 Chaniá. *Tel: (0821) 26426.*
Irakleío Tourist Office, Xanthoudidou 1,
712 02 Irakleío. Tel: (081) 228225.
Kefalloniá
Information Office of Argostóli, Provita
Teloniou Customs Office Dock.
Tel: (0671) 22248.
Lésvos
North Aegean Tourist Office, Tz.
Aristarchou 6, North Aegean Regional
Building, Mytilíni.
Tel: (0251) 42511.

Rhodes
Tourist Office of the Dodecanese, Arch
Makariou and Papagou, 851 00 Rhodes.
Tel: (0241) 23655.
Sámos
Sámos Information Office, 25 Martiou
4, 831 00 Sámos. *Tel: (0273) 28582.*
Sýros
Ermoúpoli Information Office,
Town Hall, Ermoúpoli 841 00.
Tel: (0281) 22375.

Travellers with Disabilities
Facilities for disabled travellers in the
Greek islands are poor. Hotel lifts
(where available) are often too small for
wheelchairs, and ramps are extremely
rare. Sidewalks, where they exist, are
narrow and uneven, and roads often
deeply potholed. Most island sites are
atop steep hills. Before leaving the UK,
contact RADAR, 25 Mortimer Street,
London W1N 8AB (*tel: (020) 7637 5400*)
and the Holiday Care Service (*tel: (012)
9377 4535*) for general help and advice.

Leisurely hours under the sun

ACKNOWLEDGEMENTS
The Automobile Association wishes to thank the following organizations, libraries and photographers for their
assistance in the preparation of this book.

CHRISTINE OSBORNE PICTURES 36, 37, 84, 102a, 106, 153, 158, 160, 161, 182, 183, 184
M CRAME/CHRISTINE OSBORNE PICTURES 78
NATURE PHOTOGRAPHERS 42a
NEIL SETCHFIELD 8, 11, 13, 15, 21, 146, 156, 157b, 175, 179, 189
PICTURES COLOUR LIBRARY 27, 39, 79, 140, 141, 149, 169
SPECTRUM COLOUR LIBRARY 14b, 57, 139, 144, 145a, 145b, 162, 164, 165, 166a, 168
THE TRAVEL LIBRARY 24a, 33, 46a, 65
J ARNOLD/jonarnold.com back cover top left and centre

The remaining pictures are held in the AA PHOTO LIBRARY and were taken by: STEVE DAY 6, 7, 22, 70, 86, 87, 89,
91, 92, 93, 94, 95, 96, 97, 98, 99, 100a, 100b, 101, 102b, 104, 105, 107, 108a, 108b, 110, 130a, 130b, 131b,
151, 154a, 154b, 163, 167, 170b, 172, 178, 186, 187; KEN PATTERSON 14a, 19, 81, 83, 109b, 148b, 159, 166b;
P ENTICKNAP 80, 131a, 157a; P WILSON 46b, 51, 148a, 171; TERRY HARRIS back cover top right, 16, 17, 55, 59, 60,
61, 63, 64, 66, 67, 68, 69, 71, 72, 74, 75, 77, 170a, 174, 176, 180; JAMES TIMS 18, 24b, 28, 29, 30, 31, 34, 35, 48,
49, 50, 177; R MOORE 20, 132a, 132b, 134, 135, 136, 137, 142, 143, 147; A SATTIN 23, 41, 42b, 45, 109a, 114,
115, 116, 117, 119, 120, 121, 123, 125, 126, 127, 129, 173.

FOR LABURNUM TECHNOLOGIES

Design Director	Alpana Khare	**Photo Editor**	Radhika Singh
Series Director	Razia Grover	**DTP Designers**	Neeraj Aggarwal,
Editors	Madhumadhavi Singh,		Harish Aggarwal
	Rajiv Jayaram, Deepshikha Singh		

Updating and additional research on this edition was done by Ioannis Karkanis.
Thanks to Marie Lorimer for the Index.

Travellers

Feedback Form

Please help us improve future editions by taking part in our reader survey. Every returned form will be acknowledged. To show our appreciation we will send you a voucher entitling you to £1 off your next *Travellers* guide or any other Thomas Cook guidebook ordered direct from Thomas Cook Publishing. Just take a few minutes to complete and return this form to us.

We'd also be glad to hear of your comments, updates or recommendations on places we cover or you think that we ought to cover.

1. Which *Travellers* guide did you purchase?

_____

2. Have you purchased other *Travellers* guides in the series?

Yes ☐

No ☐

If Yes, please specify_____

3. Which of the following tempted you into buying your *Travellers* guide: (Please tick as many as appropriate)

The price ☐

The FREE weblinks CD ☐

The cover ☐

The content ☐

Other_____

4. What do you think of :

a) the cover design? _____

b) the design and layout styles within the book?_____

c) the FREE weblinks CD?_____

5. Please tell us about any features that in your opinion could be changed, improved or added in future editions of the book or CD:

_____

_____

_____

Your age category: ☐ under 21 ☐ 21-30 ☐ 31-40 ☐ 41-50 ☐ 51+

Mr/Mrs/Miss/Ms/Other

Surname_____ Initials_____

Full address: (Please include postal or zip code)_____

_____

Daytime telephone number: _____

Email address:_____

☐ Please tick here if you would be willing to participate in further customer surveys.

☐ Please tick here if you would like to receive information on new titles or special offers from Thomas Cook Publishing (please note we never give your details to third party companies).

Please detach this page and send it to: **The Editor, Travellers, Thomas Cook Publishing, PO Box 227, The Thomas Cook Business Park, Peterborough PE3 8XX, United Kingdom.**

tear along the perforation

The Editor, Travellers
Thomas Cook Publishing
PO Box 227
The Thomas Cook Business Park
Peterborough, PE3 8XX
United Kingdom